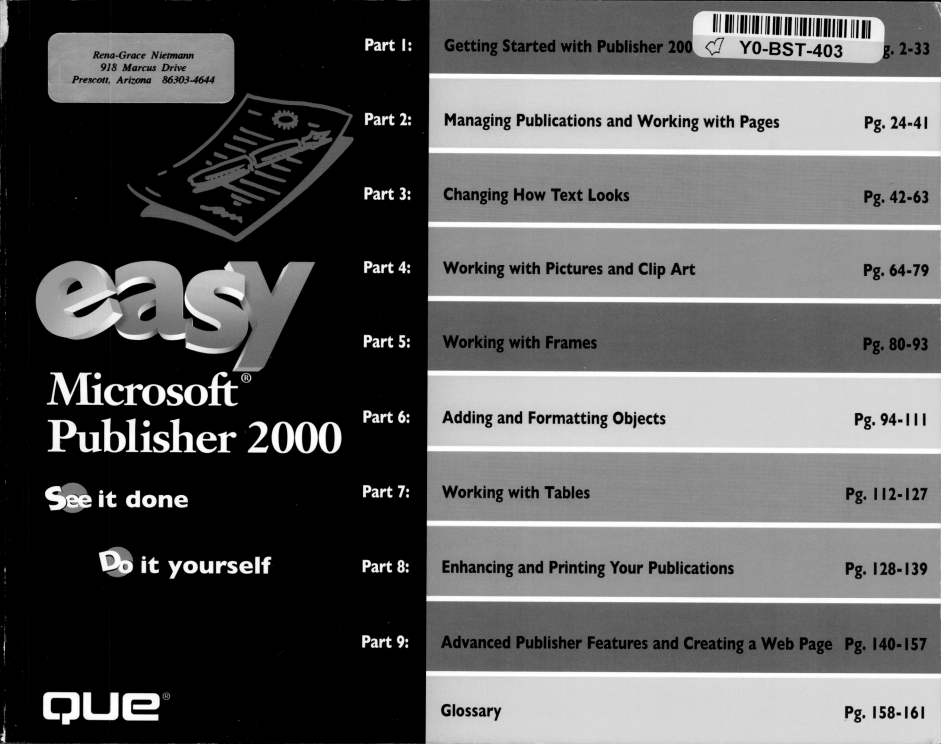

easy
Microsoft® Publisher 2000

See it done

Do it yourself

que®

Y0-BST-403

Part ▶ 8: Enhancing and Printing Your Publications

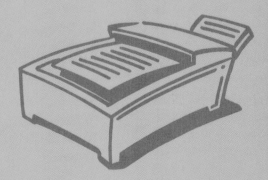

Part ▶ 9: Advanced Publisher Features and Creating a Web Page

About the Author

Joe Habraken is a computer technology professional and author with more than 14 years of experience as an educator and consultant in the information technology field. Joe is a Microsoft Certified Professional and has taught computer-software seminars across the country. He has a Masters degree from the American University in Washington, D.C., and currently serves as the lead instructor for the Networking Technologies program at Globe College in St. Paul, Minnesota. Joe's recent book titles include *The Microsoft Access 97 Exam Guide*, *The Complete Idiot's Guide to Microsoft Access 2000*, *Sams Teach Yourself Microsoft Publisher in Ten Minutes*, *Microsoft Office 2000 8-in-1*, and *Using Lotus SmartSuite Millennium Edition*.

Dedication and Acknowledgments

To my cousins Larry, Gary, Greg, Doug, and Mary—thanks for sharing your comic books when we were growing up!

I would like to thank Jamie Milazzo for pulling the team together that made this project a reality. Also a big thanks to Lisa McGowan, our development editor, who had a number of great ideas for improving the book's content, and Kyle Bryant, who made sure that everything was technically accurate.

Executive Editor
Angela Wethington

Acquisitions Editor
Jamie Milazzo

Development Editor
Lisa McGowan

Managing Editor
Lisa Wilson

Project Editor
Rebecca Mounts

Copy Editor
Cheri Clark

Indexer
Rebecca Salerno

Proofreader
Billy Fields

Technical Editor
Kyle Bryant

Interior Design
Jean Bisesi

Cover Design
Anne Jones

Layout Technicians
Lisa England
Ayanna Lacey
Heather Hiatt Miller
Amy Parker

How to Use This Book

It's as Easy as 1-2-3

Each part of this book is made up of a series of short, instructional lessons, designed to help you understand basic information that you need to get the most out of your computer hardware and software.

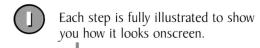

① Each step is fully illustrated to show you how it looks onscreen.

Click: Click the left mouse button once.

Double-click: Click the left mouse button twice in rapid succession.

Right-click: Click the right mouse button once.

Pointer Arrow: Highlights an item on the screen you need to point to or focus on in the step or task.

Selection: Highlights the area onscreen discussed in the step or task.

Click & Type: Click once where indicated and begin typing to enter your text or data.

✓ Tips and **①** Warnings give you a heads-up for any extra information you may need while working through the task.

② Each task includes a series of quick, easy steps designed to guide you through the procedure.

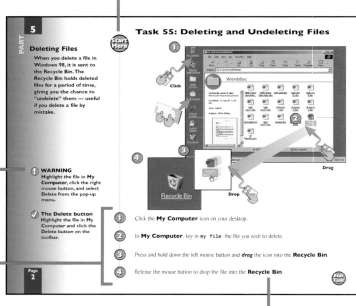

```
5  PART    Task 55: Deleting and Undeleting Files

Deleting Files
When you delete a file in
Windows 98, it is sent to
the Recycle Bin. The
Recycle Bin holds deleted
files for a period of time,
giving you the chance to
"undelete" them — useful
if you delete a file by
mistake.

① WARNING
Highlight the file in My
Computer, click the right
mouse button, and select
Delete from the pop-up
menu.

✓ The Delete button
Highlight the file in My
Computer and click the
Delete button on the
toolbar.

Page 2

① Click the My Computer icon on your desktop.
② In My Computer, key in my file the file you wish to delete.
③ Press and hold down the left mouse button and drag the icon into the Recycle Bin.
④ Release the mouse button to drop the file into the Recycle Bin.
```

③ Items that you select or click in menus, dialog boxes, tabs, and windows are shown in **Bold**. Information you type is in a **special font**.

Drag

Drop

How to Drag: Point to the starting place or object. Hold down the mouse button (right or left per instructions), move the mouse to the new location, then release the button.

Next Step: If you see this symbol, it means the task you're working on continues on the next page.

End Task: Task is complete.

Introduction to Publisher 2000

Easy Microsoft Publisher 2000 will show you how to work efficiently and effectively as you build your own publications in Publisher. This powerful yet easy-to-use desktop publishing program can be used to create brochures, business cards, and even Web sites for your small business, or to create greeting cards and other fun publications for your personal use. Whatever type of publication you want to create in Publisher, this book will get you started on the right track.

Publisher will help you create publications by using Wizards and Design Sets. You will learn how to insert and manage objects in your publications, including text frames, picture frames, and even video and sound clips. You will also learn how to print your completed publications and how to prepare them for printing by a professional printer. You will get the information you need in order to create many kinds of publications, and you will even learn to create your own Web site with Publisher.

Tell Us What You Think!

As the reader of this book, *you* are our most important critic and commentator. We value your opinion and want to know what we're doing right, what we could do better, what areas you'd like to see us publish in, and any other words of wisdom you're willing to pass our way.

As the Publisher for the General Desktop Applications team at Que Publishing, I welcome your comments. You can fax, email, or write me directly to let me know what you did or didn't like about this book—as well as what we can do to make our books stronger.

Please note that I cannot help you with technical problems related to the topic of this book, and that due to the high volume of mail I receive, I might not be able to reply to every message.

When you write, please be sure to include this book's title and author as well as your name and phone or fax number. I will carefully review your comments and share them with the author and editors who worked on the book.

Fax: 317-581-4666
Email: office_que@mcp.com
Mail: John Pierce
            Publisher
            General Desktop Applications
            201 West 103rd Street
            Indianapolis, IN 46290 USA

PART 1

Getting Started with Publisher 2000

Microsoft Publisher is a software application that makes it easy for you to create sophisticated and professional-looking personal and business publications, such as greeting cards, business cards, and brochures. Before you dive in and begin to create your own publications, however, it makes sense to discuss some of the items you will be working with.

A **publication** is the end product of your work in Publisher. A publication can be a flyer, a brochure, a set of business cards—any number of business or personal documents with special looks and layouts.

A **Wizard** is a special feature that actually walks you through the steps of creating publications in Publisher. You will work with various Wizards that are specific to certain publication types but share a common way of creating the publication.

An **object** is any item such as a picture, text box, or drawn item that you place on your publication. You will find that Publisher also provides a great deal of help when it comes to placing objects in your publications.

A **frame** is the area that an object resides in. You can format frame borders, change the color of frames, and manipulate frames in various ways.

This part of the book will help you get up and running quickly so that you can create your own publications. The topics covered are shown in the following task list.

Tasks

Task I: Starting Publisher

Opening the Publisher Window

When you install Microsoft Publisher, the program files, clip art, and other software files associated with the Publisher application are placed on your computer. A program icon for Publisher is also placed on your Windows Start menu, which you can use to open the Publisher application.

 **Starting Publisher Using a File**

If you already have a publication saved on your computer's hard drive, you can start Publisher by locating the file using Windows Explorer and then double-clicking the Publisher file. The Publisher window opens and loads the publication.

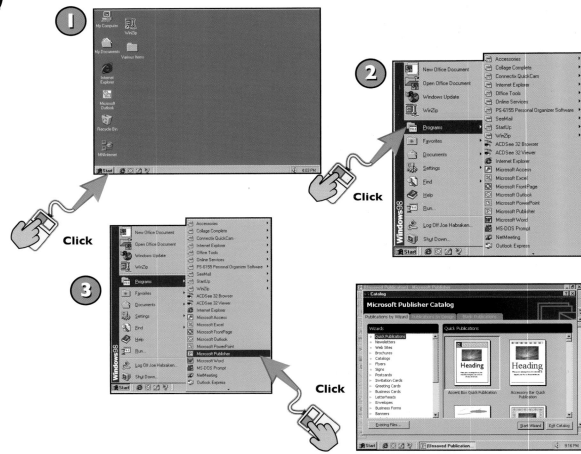

Click

Click

Click

① Click the Windows **Start** button.

② Point at **Programs** on the Start menu.

③ Choose **Publisher** on the cascading menu. The Publisher window opens on the Windows desktop.

Task 2: Editing Your Personal Information

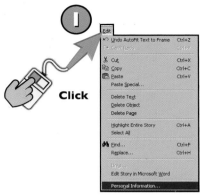

Click

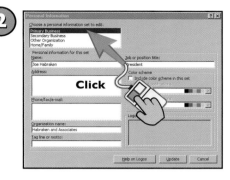

Click

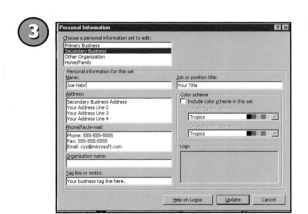

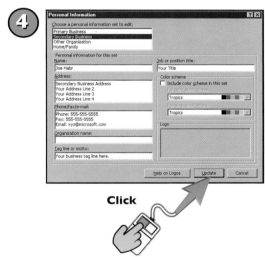

Click

Providing Your Publications with Information

Whether you create a new publication using a Wizard or a Design Set or start from scratch, Publisher can automatically place information in the publication from your personal information sets. These sets (**Primary Business, Secondary Business, Other Organization,** and **Home/Family**) contain information such as your name and company name which can be inserted into the text boxes your publications.

✓ **The Wizards Give You a Chance to Edit Your Information Sets**
When you use a publication Wizard, it gives you a chance to revise the data in the four information sets. After you edit a set, you can then select it for the current publication.

① With a publication open in Publisher, choose **Edit, Personal Information**. The Personal Information dialog box appears.

② Choose the information set you want to edit in the **Choose a personal information set to edit** box (such as **Secondary Business**).

③ Click in the various text boxes and edit the current information they contain (or fill in any blanks).

④ When you have completed editing the information set, choose another set to edit, or click the **Update** button to close the dialog box.

Page
5

Understanding the Publisher Catalog

When you open the Publisher application, the first thing that appears is the *Publisher Catalog.* You can quickly begin a new publication from within the Catalog by using either a Publication Wizard or a Design Set, or by creating a blank presentation from a *template.*

✓ First Publication

The simplest way to create your first publication is by using the **Publications by Wizard** tab on the Publisher Catalog window. After you select a particular publication, the Wizard walks you through the steps of choosing the various color schemes and design elements for the publication.

Task 3: Starting a New Publication with a Wizard

Start Here

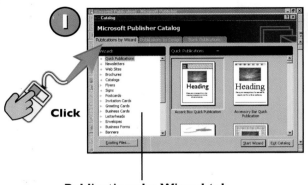

Publications by Wizard tab

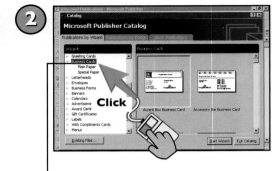

Publication category

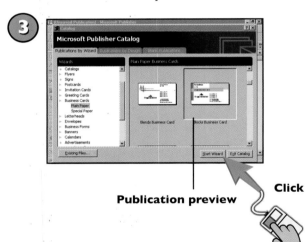

Publication preview

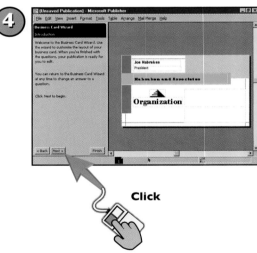

Click

Click

1. Choose the **Publications by Wizard** tab on the Catalog window.

2. Choose a category in the Wizards pane and then choose the publication you want to create in the Preview window.

3. Click the **Start Wizard** button to create the selected publication. The publication appears in the Publication window.

4. The Wizard for the selected publication appears in the left pane; click **Next** to continue.

Next Step

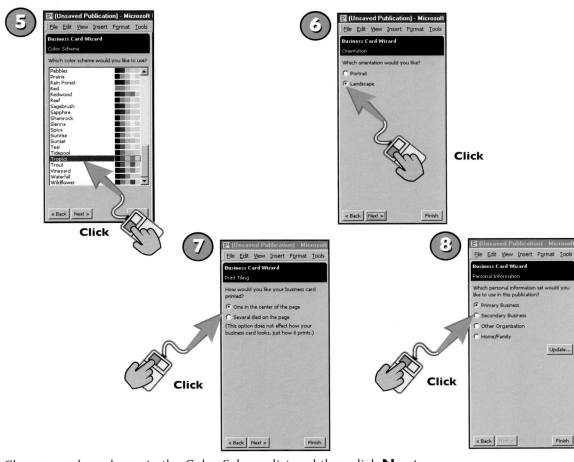

Click

Click

Click

Click

Completing the Publication

When you click **Finish**, the Wizard gives you control of the publication. You may use the Publisher toolbars and menu system to edit and enhance your publication.

✓ Page Orientation
Portrait orientation is used for a standard sheet of paper, 8 1/2 by 11 inches (where height is greater than width). Rotate the page 90 degrees and you have Landscape orientation.

✓ Wizard Steps May Vary
The number of steps it takes the Wizard to complete a publication may vary from those outlined here.

✓ The Wizards Supply Placeholders
In many cases the Wizard will put *placeholders* on your publication. These placeholders can hold pictures and other design elements such as a company logo. The intent of the placeholders is that you will place your own design or company logo in the area that holds the generic placeholder object.

(5) Choose a color scheme in the Color Scheme list and then click **Next**.

(6) Click either the **Portrait** or **Landscape** radio button to orient your publication, and then click **Next** to continue.

(7) After determining whether you want a logo placeholder (by clicking **Next**), click a radio button to determine how your publication will be printed and then click **Next**.

(8) Choose the personal information set you want to use to supply information for the publication, and then click **Finish**.

End Task

Using Design Sets

Publisher provides you with a way to create sets of publications that share the same color and design attributes. This makes it easy for you to create small business publications such as business cards, envelopes, brochures, and letterheads that share the same look.

Task 4: Creating Publications with a Unified Design

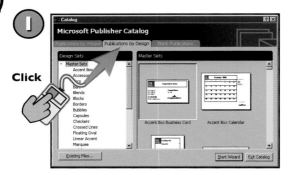

Click

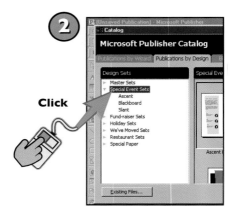

Click

Click

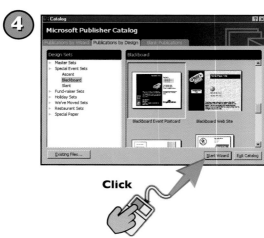

Click

✅ **Opening the Publisher Catalog**

If you have already been working in the Publisher window and want to open the Publisher Catalog, choose **File, New**. The New button on the toolbar opens a new blank publication but does not open the Catalog.

(1) Choose the **Publications by Design** tab on the Catalog window.

(2) Choose one of the design sets in the Design Sets pane (for example, **Special Event Sets**).

(3) Choose a publication in the Preview window (such as **Blackboard Event Postcard**).

(4) Click the **Start Wizard** button to begin the creation of your publication.

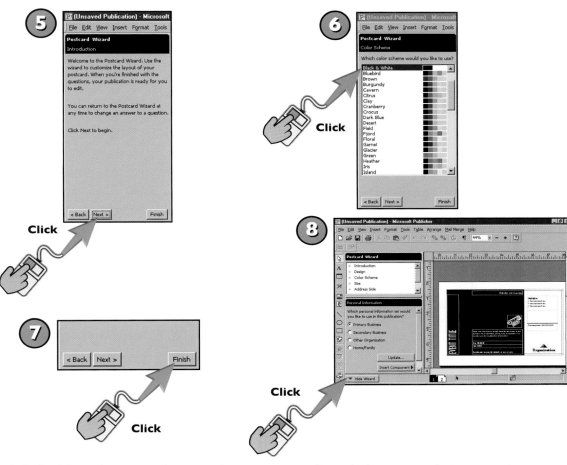

Remember that when you create a publication using a Design Set, your ultimate purpose is to create a family of publications that have the same look and feel. If you change some of the design parameters, such as color scheme, for a particular publication, make sure that you make the same changes to other publications that will be part of the publication group.

Remember to Click Finish

The Wizard controls the changes to your publication until you click the Finish button. You can then use the menu system and toolbars to change the look of your new publication.

(5) Click the **Next** button in the Wizard pane to move through the various design questions posed by the Wizard.

(6) Choose design parameters such as the publication's Color Scheme, and then click **Next** to continue.

(7) Click **Finish** when you have made the design choices offered by the Wizard. Your completed publication appears in the Publication window.

(8) If you want more room to work on your new publication, click the **Hide Wizard** button to close the Wizard pane.

Task 5: Creating a Blank Publication

Designing Publications from Scratch

If you find that designing publications using the Wizard or Design Sets restricts your creativity, you can also design publications from scratch using a blank publication. Publisher does provide help, however, even with blank publications.

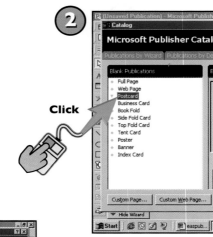

Click

Click

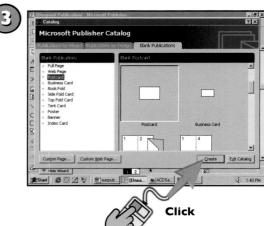

Click

✓ **Blank Publication Templates**

When you create a blank publication, Publisher provides you with a template that sets up the page layout for your new publication. You can choose templates for blank publications in the Publication Preview window.

1. Choose the **Blank Publications** tab on the Publisher Catalog.

2. Choose a blank publication template in the Publication Preview window.

3. To create the selected blank publication, click **Create**. The publication opens in the Preview window, and the Quick Publication Wizard appears in the Wizard pane.

Selecting Blank Publication Design Elements

You can use the Quick Publication Wizard to change any of the design parameters on your blank publication, including design elements, color scheme, page size, and layout.

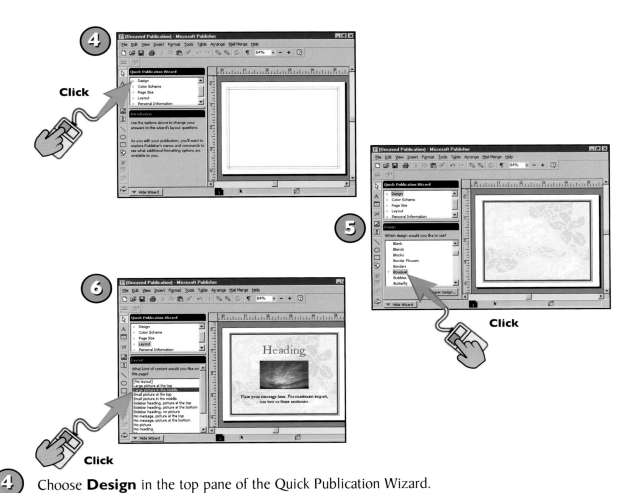

Click

Click

Click

(4) Choose **Design** in the top pane of the Quick Publication Wizard.

(5) Choose a design from the lower pane of the Quick Publication Wizard (such as **Bouquet**).

(6) Choose other design, color, and layout parameters as needed (for instance, choose a layout for the publication).

 **Using Layout for Placeholders**

To automatically put placeholders on your blank publication, choose the **Layout** heading in the Quick Publication Wizard pane, and choose one of the ready-made designs that includes placeholders for pictures and other design elements.

 End Task

Getting Your Publisher Geography Down

Although much of your work in Publisher is initially driven by Wizards, there are various tools and areas of the Publisher window that you will work with as you enhance or edit your publications. Publisher is a typical Microsoft application that enables you to manipulate the window you are working in.

Task 6: Understanding the Publisher Work Area

Click

✓ **Taking Charge of the Publisher Window**
You can increase the size of the work area for your publication in the Publisher window. To do so, click the **Hide Wizard** button to remove the current Wizard.

1. Click the application window buttons (**Minimize**, **Maximize**, **Close**) to alter the size of (or close) the Publisher window.

2. Click the arrows on the scrollbars to scroll in that direction, or drag the scroll box up or down.

3. Click the **Page** buttons on the status bar to move from page to page in your publication.

Next Step

Ruler tick marks

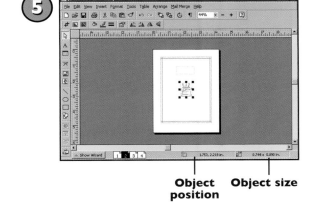

Ruler tick marks

The Publisher Window Is Designed for Objects

When you work with your publications, the name of the game is really placing and enhancing objects (such as text boxes, pictures, and other design elements) on your publication pages. The Publisher status bar and rulers are designed to help you place and size your objects appropriately.

Click

Object position   **Object size**

(4) Watch the tick marks on the rulers to position an object on a publication page by drawing with the mouse.

(5) Use the status bar to view the position and size of a selected object in a publication.

(6) Click the **Show Wizard** button to get help from the current publication Wizard.

 Maximizing the Publisher Window
To give you the maximum amount of workspace by maximizing the Publisher window, click the Maximize button.

Task 7: Working with Menus

Using the Personalized Menus

The menu bar is just below the title bar in the Publisher window. All the commands available to you in Publisher can be selected from the various menus. Publisher 2000 and Microsoft Office 2000 embrace a new menu system called *Personalized* menus. The Personalized menus "adapt" to your use of commands and show your most-recently used commands first. Infrequently used commands are hidden, but if you hold the menu open for a moment by the double chevron marker at the bottom of the menu, all the available commands appear. As you use a new command in the personalized environment, it joins the other recently used commands at the top of the menu list.

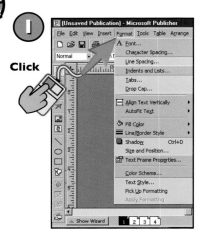

Click

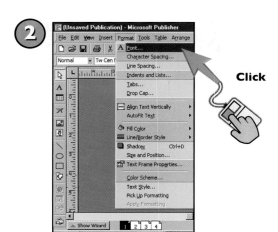

Click

Drop-down list box

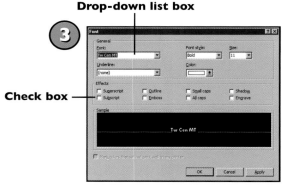

Check box

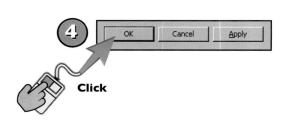

Click

To open a menu, choose the menu name (for example, **Format**, when text is selected).

Choose the command you want to use on the menu (such as **Font**). Menu commands marked with an ellipsis open a dialog box.

Use the drop-down boxes, check boxes, radio buttons, and text boxes to make your selection in the dialog box.

Click the **OK** button to close the dialog box.

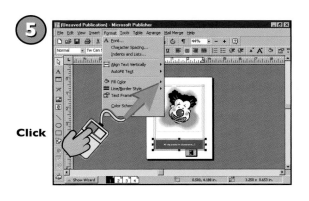

Click

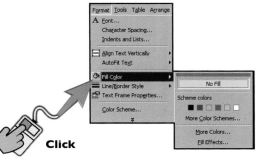

Click

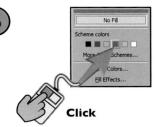

Click

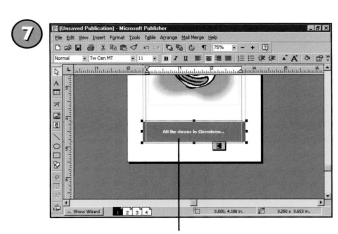

New red fill color

⑤ Menu commands marked with a triangle open a cascading menu of additional choices or a command box (such as the **Fill Color** command, available when an object is selected).

⑥ Choose a color on the Color palette that appears.

⑦ The color palette disappears, and the command takes effect in your publication.

Undo Unwanted Commands

You can easily undo any command that you decide not to execute. Choose **Edit, Undo.** The command is undone. Then if you decide you want it after all, you can choose **Edit, Redo.**

✓ Turning Off the Personalized Menus
If you want to turn off the Personalized menu system and use the standard menus, choose **Tools, Options.** On the General tab of the Options dialog box, deselect the **Menus show recently used commands first** check box.

✓ Command Availability
"Grayed out" menu commands are not available. Often you must perform a particular action in order for them to become available.

✓ Closing a Menu
To close a menu, click on the menu title or outside the menu or press the **Esc** key.

End Task

Task 8: Working with Toolbars

Working with the Publisher Toolbars

Publisher provides you with three toolbars. The Standard toolbar provides easy access to commands such as Save and Open. The Formatting toolbar makes it easy for you to format objects in your publications. The Publisher toolbar contains tools that allow you to insert and create objects for your publications.

Standard toolbar

Formatting toolbar

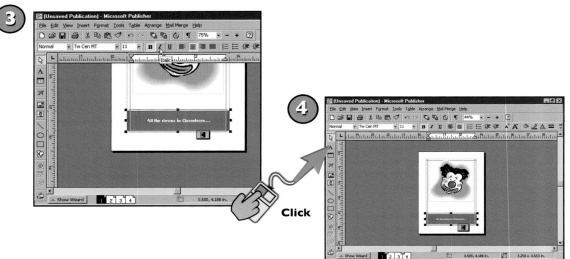

Click

✓ **Toolbar Customization**
To access additional commands on the Formatting toolbar, click the **More buttons** command on the far-right side of the toolbar.

① Place the mouse pointer on any of the buttons on the Standard toolbar (such as **Save**). A ScreenTip appears, showing the command associated with that particular button.

② To view the entire Formatting toolbar, choose an object (such as a text frame) in your publication.

③ Place the mouse pointer on any of the Formatting toolbar buttons to view a ScreenTip (such as **Center**).

④ To execute a command on a toolbar (such as the Publisher toolbar), click the button. Some buttons require that you draw an object on the page.

Next Step

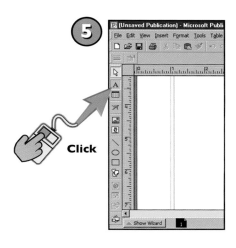

Click

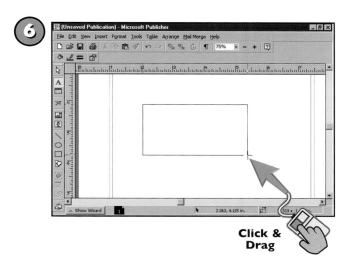

Click &
Drag

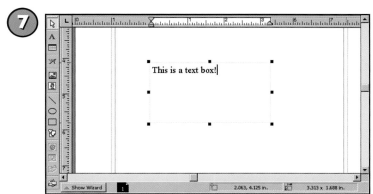

This is a text box!

The Publisher Toolbar Requires Mouse Skills

The Publisher toolbar provides you with a quick way to insert objects into your publications. You can insert text boxes, insert pictures, and draw various items. To place an object in a publication using the buttons on the Publisher toolbar, you must click a button and then use the mouse to "draw" the frame that the object will reside in.

✓ **Working with Objects**
Placing objects on your publications manually may take some practice as you nurture your own design sense. For more about working with objects, particularly drawing objects, see Part 6, "Adding and Formatting Objects."

⑤ Click a button on the Publisher toolbar (such as the **Text Frame** tool).

⑥ Place the mouse pointer on your publication, hold down the left mouse button, and drag the mouse to create an object frame.

⑦ In the case of a text frame, you can now type the text you want to place in the new text object.

End Task

Using Shortcut Menus

When you right-click an object in a publication, a *shortcut menu* appears. Shortcut menus include other commands directly related to the selected object. So each shortcut menu will vary, depending on your selection. Shortcut menus allow you to quickly access certain commands so that you don't have to search the menu system or the toolbar buttons.

✓ Cascading Shortcut Menus

Some shortcut menus provide choices that contain cascading menus. When you point at a menu command marked with an arrow, a secondary, cascading menu appears. Make your choice on the cascading menu.

✓ Closing a Shortcut Menu

Click anywhere in the Publisher window or press the Esc key to close.

Task 9: Taking Advantage of Shortcut Menus

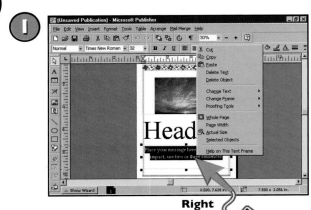

Right Click

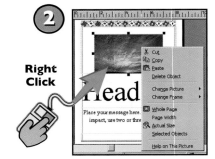

Right Click

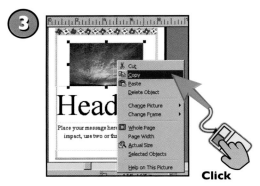

Click

1 In any publication, right-click a text frame to view the shortcut menu.

2 Right-click a picture or clip art object to view the shortcut menu.

3 Choose a particular command on the shortcut menu (such as **Copy**), and the menu disappears when the command is executed.

Task 10: Getting Help from the Office Assistant

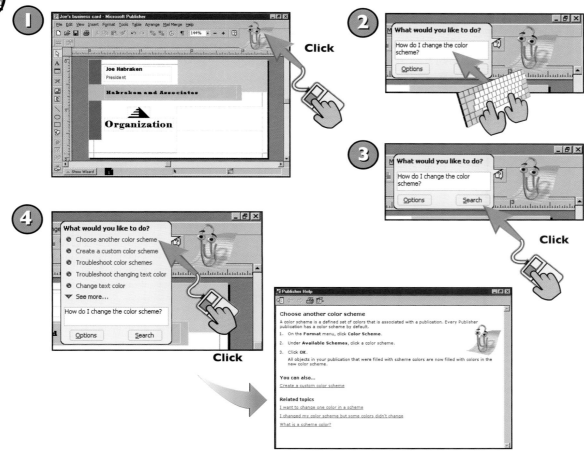

Click

Working with the Office Assistant

If you need publications help, the Office Assistant is always available. Ask it a question and it provides you with options related to your particular need, such as context-sensitive help on the task you are executing. Just watch the Assistant and when a light bulb appears over its head, click the Assistant for help.

✓ **Finding the Assistant**
If the Assistant isn't in the Publisher window, click the **Help** button on the Standard toolbar, then choose **Help, Show the Office Assistant.**

✓ **Hiding the Assistant checkbox**
If you want to temporarily hide the **Office Assistant,** right-click on the Assistant and then choose **Hide** on the shortcut menu.

1 Click the **Office Assistant**.

2 Type your question in the Assistant's Balloon (for example, **How do I change the color scheme?**).

3 Click the **Search** button to search the Help system for topics related to your question.

4 Choose any of the topics that appear in the Assistant's Balloon (such as **Choose another color scheme**). The Publisher Help window opens with help on that topic.

Task 11: Getting Help Using the Help System

Going Directly to the Help System

If you find that you don't like using the Office Assistant, you can go directly to the Publisher Help system to get the help you need. The Help system provides you with three ways to look up information: you can use the Contents tab, which divides help into broad topics; the Answer Wizard, which allows you to ask questions to find help (like the Office Assistant); or the Index tab, which allows you to look for help by searching with keywords.

✓ Turning Off the Office Assistant

To directly access the Publisher Help system without going through the Office Assistant, turn the Assistant off. Right-click on the Assistant and choose **Options** on the shortcut menu. In the Options dialog box, click the **Use the Office Assistant** check box to clear the option.

Start Here

Click

Click

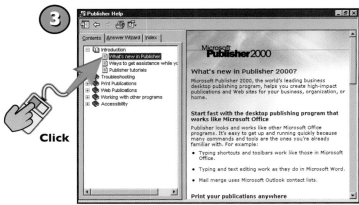

Click

1 Choose **Help**, **Microsoft Publisher Help** to open the Publisher Help system.

2 On the Contents tab, click any of the plus symbols to the left of the topics (they look like books) to expand one of the topics (such as **Introduction**).

3 Choose one of the subtopics under the Introduction heading. The information related to that topic appears in the right pane of the Help window.

Next Step

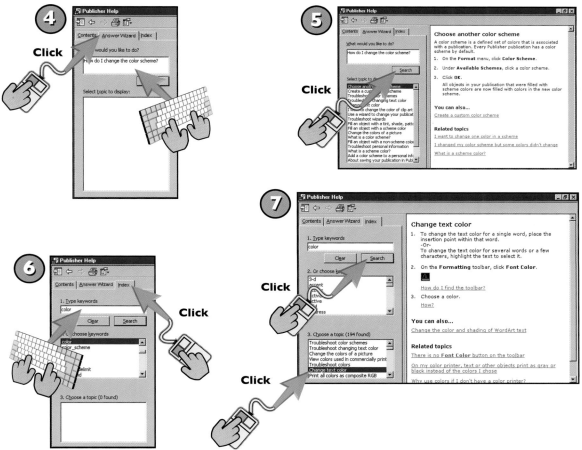

Using the Answer Wizard and the Index

The Help window provides two other ways of getting help: the **Answer Wizard** and the **Index**. The Answer Wizard allows you to ask a question and then provides a list of topics related to your question. The Index searches for information using keywords you type into the Index box.

 Minimizing the Help window

Remember that you can use the **Minimize** button on the Help window to temporarily remove that window from the desktop so that you can see your publication in the Publisher window.

---

4 Choose the **Answer Wizard** tab and type your question in the **What would you like to do?** box.

5 Click **Search** to view a list of help topics; choose any topic to view the help information.

6 Choose the **Index** tab and type a keyword in the **Type Keywords** box.

7 Click the **Search** button to retrieve a list of topics related to the keyword. Choose any topic to view related information in the right pane of the Help window.

Using What's This? Help

At times you will need additional information on a certain option or feature before you can make your selections in a particular dialog box. You can get fast information by using the What's This? mouse pointer. When you click on a particular item using this feature, you get information on the area of the dialog box you selected.

ⓘ Warning

Some dialog boxes do not provide a helpful What's This? box when you click on an area. In this case, the pop-up says, "No Help ... with this item." Then you will have to use the Help system or the Office Assistant.

✓ Closing the Dialog Box

If you open a dialog box but don't make any changes to the settings it provides, click the **Cancel** button to close it.

Task 12: Getting Help on Dialog Box Items

Start Here

Click

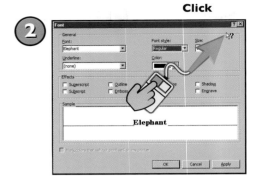

Click

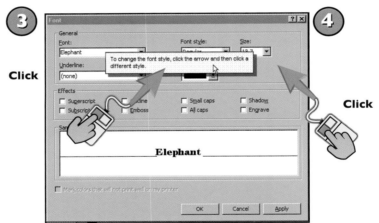

Click   Click

Click

(1) Open any dialog box (such as the Font dialog box—choose **Format**, **Font**).

(2) Click the **What's This?** button in the upper-right corner of the dialog box. The mouse pointer becomes a question mark.

(3) Click on a specific area of the dialog box (such as the **Font style** box). A pop-up box appears with information related to the area of the dialog box you clicked on.

(4) Click anywhere in the dialog box to close the pop-up box.

End Task

Task 13: Exiting Publisher

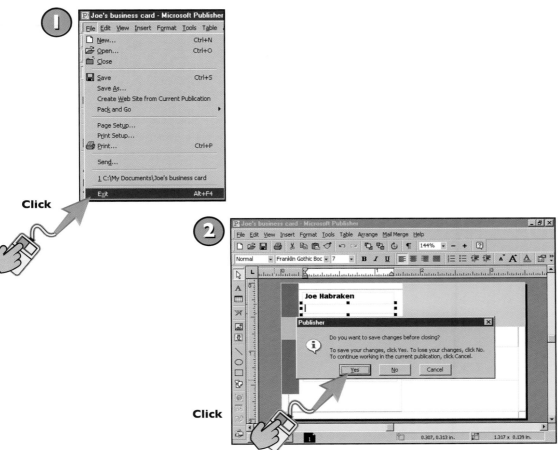

Click

Click

Providing Your Publications with Information

When you've finished working on a publication or publications, you will probably want to close the Publisher window so that you can work on other tasks or exit Windows completely. You will be prompted to save any work you've inadvertently forgotten to save to your computer (for more about saving your publications, see "Saving a Publication" in Part 2, "Managing Publications and Working with Pages").

① Choose **File**, **Exit**.

② Click **Yes** to save your work if you are prompted; then the Publisher window closes.

✓ **Clicking the Close Button to Exit Publisher**
You can also exit Publisher by clicking the **Close** button on the right side of the Publisher title bar.

Managing Publications and Working with Pages

As you work in Publisher and create various publications using the Wizards and Design Sets, you will find that managing and editing the publications is as important as creating them. You will no doubt want to be able to open existing publications and then enhance the publications by adding pages, page numbers, and other items. For example, you may create a floor plan that will eventually span several pages. As you work on this publication, you will want to save changes you make and also be able to open the file later if you want to make more changes. You will also want to be able to view your publication and zoom in and out on pages in such a way that editing text and pictures is easy. And understanding how to accurately place new items (such as text frames or picture frames) on a specific area of the page is also a must for great-looking publications.

Tasks

Task 1: Saving a Publication

Saving Your Publications to Disk

Saving your publications is a necessity. When you create a new publication in Publisher, the publication exists only in your computer's memory. Until you actually save the file to your hard disk or a floppy disk, you haven't insured your work against loss. "Save it or lose it" should really be your mantra as you work in Publisher.

✓ **Publisher Prompts You to Save**
After creating a new publication, you will find that Publisher will prompt you on occasion to save changes you have made to the publication. Click the **Yes** button in the dialog box that appears to save your file.

✓ **Save As Command**
To save the publication under a new filename, choose **File, Save As.** Type the new filename in the Save As dialog box, then click **Save** to save the file.

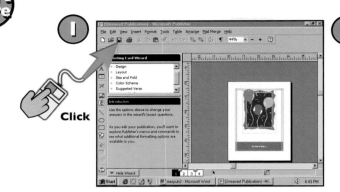

Click

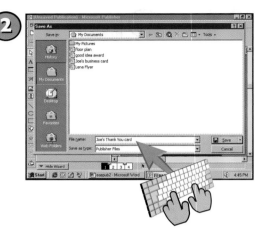

Double-Click

Click

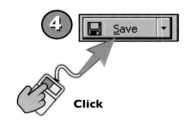

Click

① With your publication open in Publisher, click the **Save** button on the Standard toolbar.

② Type a filename in the File name box of the Save As dialog box.

③ Click the arrow on the **Save in** drop-down box to select a drive, and then double-click the appropriate folder that will hold the file.

④ Click the **Save** button in the Save As dialog box. The title bar now contains your publication's name.

Task 2: Opening a Publication

Start Here

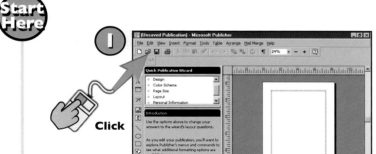

Click

Double-Click

Click

Click

Working with Saved Files

You will probably find that you end up with a "library" of saved publications you use on a fairly regular basis. Items such as certificates, invitation cards, and various business forms can be created and saved to your computer and then used when needed. The great thing about recycling publications in this way is that you take the time to design them well once, and then you can open and edit them to fit your particular need.

✓ **Open Existing Publications**
If you have just started Microsoft Publisher, you can open existing files by clicking the **Existing Files** button on the **Publisher Catalog**. This action opens the **Open Publication** dialog box.

---

(1) Click the **Open** button on the Standard toolbar.

(2) In the Open Publication dialog box, click the arrow on the **Look in** drop-down box to specify the drive on which the publication you want to open resides.

(3) Double-click the folder that contains the file.

(4) Choose the file you want to open, and then click the **Open** button.

End Task

Task 3: Adding Pages to a Publication

Placing New Pages in the Publication

You will probably find that when you create complex publications (typically things you create from scratch) you may need to add additional pages to the publication itself. Publisher makes it easy for you to add a page before or after the current publication page (the one currently shown in the Publisher window).

Inserting Pages with Ready-Made Frames

When you insert new pages into your publication using the Insert Page dialog box, you can choose to create a text frame on each of the pages you insert or to duplicate all the items (text frames, picture frames, and so on) on the current page by clicking the appropriate radio button.

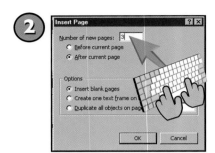

Click

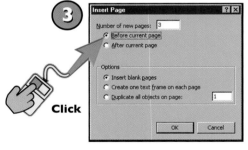

Click

Click

① Choose **Insert**, **Page**.

② Type the number of new pages you want in the Number of new pages box.

③ Click either the **Before current page** or the **After current page** radio button to position the new page or pages.

④ Click the **OK** button to insert the new page or pages.

Task 4: Deleting a Page

Start Here

1

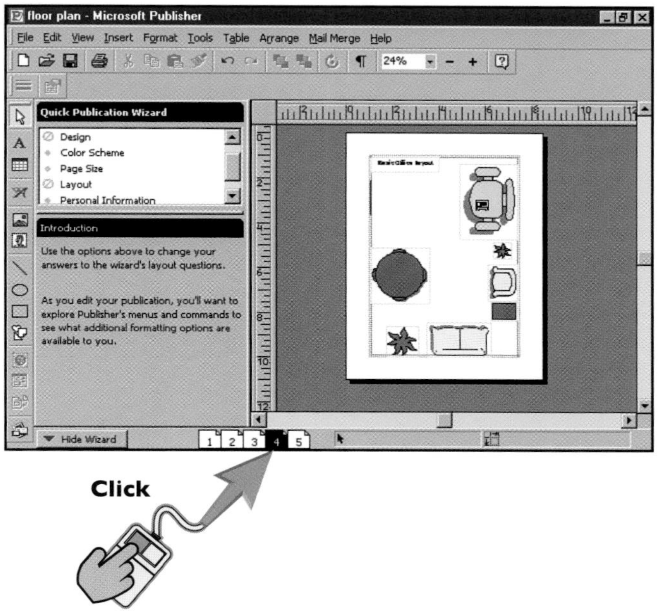

2

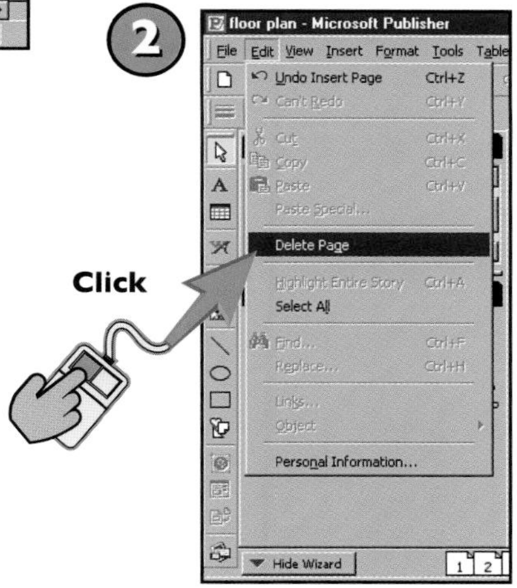

1 Click the appropriate page button on the Publisher Taskbar to select the page to be deleted.

2 Choose **Edit**, **Delete Page**. The page is removed from the publication.

Removing Unwanted Pages

Publisher makes it easy for you to delete an unwanted page from your publication. Removing a particular page also deletes all the objects contained on the page. When you use the Delete Page command you are deleting the active page, meaning the current page in the Publisher window.

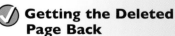

Getting the Deleted Page Back

If you inadvertently delete a page, choose **Edit, Undo Delete Page** to undo the page deletion and return the page to the publication.

End Task

Task 5: Changing the View

Using Different Page Views

When you create publications in the Publisher window, the default view is the *Whole Page view.* This allows you to see the entire current page from a sort of bird's-eye view that is excellent for determining the overall layout of the page and the positioning of the various text frames, picture frames, and other objects. The *Two-Page Spread* view allows you to examine how two *facing pages* are balanced in reference to each other.

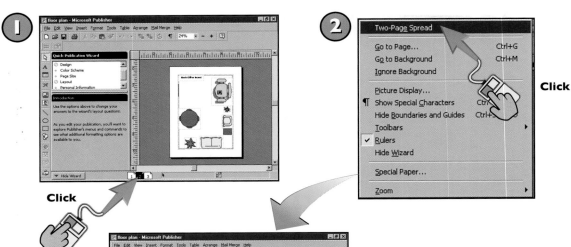

Click

Click

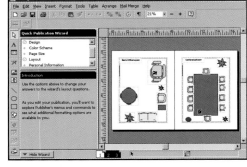

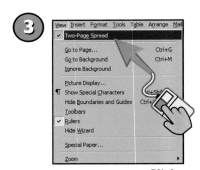

Click

Jump to Whole Page View

You can quickly go to the Whole Page view by pressing **Ctrl+Shift+L** on the keyboard.

① To switch to the Two-Page Spread view, choose a page in the publication that would have a facing page (such as page 2).

② Choose **View**, **Two-Page Spread**. A two-page spread appears.

③ To return to the Whole Page view, choose **View**, **Two-Page Spread** to deselect this option.

Next
Step

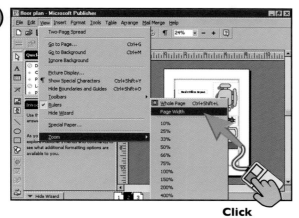

Click

Using the Page Width View

The *Page Width view* allows you to zoom in on the publication page but still see the left and right margins. This provides a screen that is slightly larger than zooming to 50% (58%) which maintains the total width of the page.

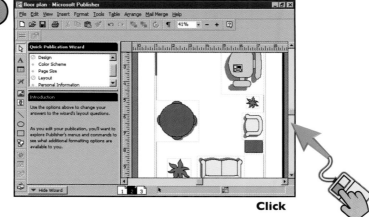

Click

✅ **View More of Your Pages**

To use the entire Publisher window to view a page or pages in a publication, click the **Hide Wizard** button to remove the current Wizard from the Publisher window.

✅ **Maximize the Publisher Window**

Make sure that the Publisher window is maximized on the Windows desktop to get the most amount of space available for viewing your publication pages. Click the **Maximize** button in the upper-right corner of the Publisher window if needed.

 To switch to the Page Width view, make sure that you are in the Whole Page view; then choose the **View** menu, point at **Zoom**, and then choose **Page Width**.

(5) Use the vertical scrollbar to view the portion of the current page you want to see (moving up or down on the page).

Task 6: Zooming In and Out

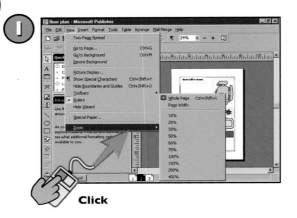

Click

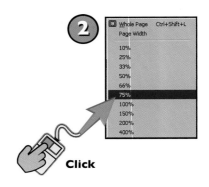

Click

Understanding the Zoom Feature

Because your publication pages will consist of various frames containing text and other items such as pictures, you will often need to edit or otherwise fine-tune these items, and you will want to be able to zoom in on them. Publisher enables you to zoom in and out on your publication pages using a range from 10% to 400% (the larger the percentage, the more you've zoomed in on your publication).

✓ **Zoom in Any View**
You can zoom in and out on your publication pages in the Whole Page view, the Two-Page Spread view, and the Page Width view.

✓ **Zoom on the Standard Toolbar**
You can also zoom in and out on your publication by using the Zoom drop-down arrow on the Publisher Standard toolbar.

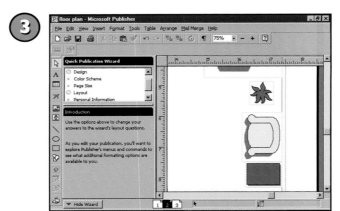

1 Choose the **View** menu and then point at **Zoom**.

2 Choose the Zoom percentage you want to use on the cascading menu.

3 Repeat the preceding steps to change the Zoom percentage or to return to one of the standard views (such as **Whole Page** view).

Task 7: Moving on and Between Pages

Start Here

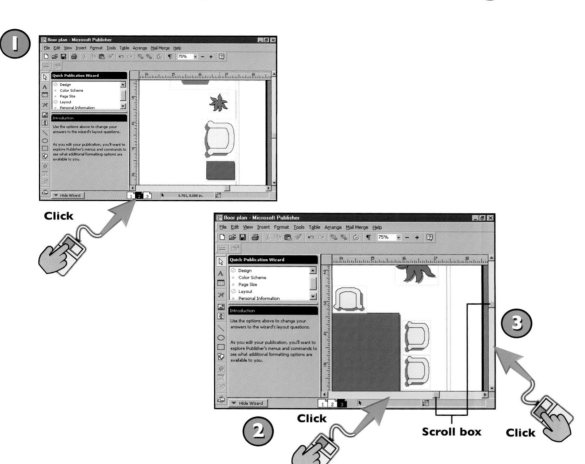

Click

Click

②

Scroll box

Click

③

Click

Selecting a Page and Scrolling on a Page

After you've zoomed in (or out) on a particular page, you may want to adjust your point of view up or down or sideways to see a particular part of the page. The vertical and horizontal scrollbars enable you to do this. If you want to be able to move from page to page in the publication, just use the page buttons on the Taskbar.

✓ **Drag the Scroll Boxes**
You can use the scroll boxes in the scrollbars to move to a spot in the document. For instance, to scroll halfway down a page, drag the vertical scroll box to the middle of the vertical scrollbar.

✓ **Go to Whole Page View for Perspective**
If you've zoomed in but can't find a particular object on the page, go back to Whole Page view to gain some perspective on that and then zoom back in.

① Click a page button (such as **page 3**) on the Publisher Taskbar to move to that page.

② Use the horizontal scrollbar to move to the left or right on the page.

③ Use the vertical scrollbar to move up or down on the page.

End Task

Task 8: Setting Ruler and Grid Guides

Taking Advantage of Guides

Placing *frames* (containing objects) on your pages is important to building any publication. Publisher lets you create nonprinting guide lines to place on your pages. Two types of guides can be created: *ruler guides* (appearing only on the page where you create them) and *grid guides* (appearing on every page, no matter where you create them on).

✓ **Clearing Ruler Guides**
To clear all ruler guides from a publication page, choose the **Arrange** menu, point at **Ruler Guides**, and then choose **Clear All Ruler Guides**.

✓ **Placing Your Own Ruler Guides**
For additional vertical guides, place the mouse on the vertical ruler, hold down the **Shift** key, and drag a guide line onto the page. Do the same for a horizontal guide.

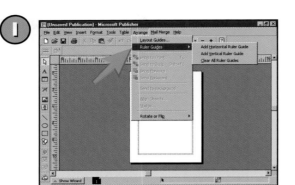

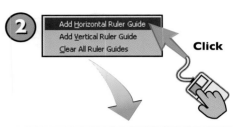

Click

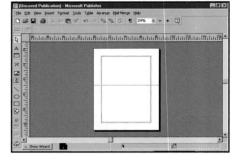

Click

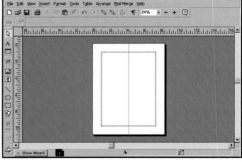

① To place ruler guides on the publication page, choose the **Arrange** menu and then point at **Ruler Guides**.

② On the cascading menu choose **Add Horizontal Ruler Guide** to place a horizontal guide.

③ Or choose **Add Vertical Ruler Guide** to add a vertical guide to the page.

Next Step

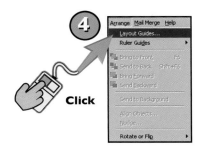

Click

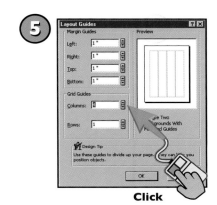

Placing Grid Guides

If you would like additional guides on your page, you can add grid guides. Grid guides are very similar to Ruler guides and are also nonprinting vertical and horizontal lines placed on the publication page. Guides help you accurately place objects such as text frames and pictures.

Click

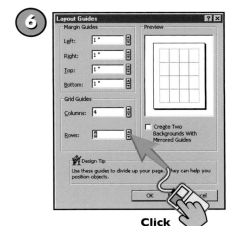

Click

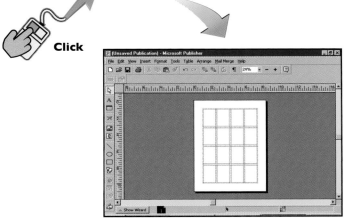

Click

✓ Changing Guides

To change or remove the column or row guides on the page, choose **Arrange, Layout Guides.** Use the arrows on the **Column** or **Row** boxes to change the number of guides, or return each box value to 1 to remove all the column or row guides.

✓ Moving Guides

To move a guide on the page, place the mouse on the guide and then hold down the **Shift** key. An adjust pointer appears. Drag the guide to a new location and then release the **Shift** key and the mouse button.

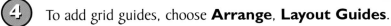

④ To add grid guides, choose **Arrange**, **Layout Guides**.

⑤ Click the arrows on the **Columns** box to specify the number of guide columns (lines) you want to place on the page.

⑥ Click the arrows on the **Rows** box to specify the number of guide rows (lines) you want to place on the page.

⑦ Click **OK**.

End Task

Task 9: Using Snap to It

Snapping Your Frames to a Guide

Snap to It is a feature supplied by Publisher that makes it easy to align objects. With this feature, the object snaps to a particular guide or another object, meaning it aligns itself at the guide or object. For instance, when you drag a text frame to a particular position on the page, you can place it near a particular guide line, and then it will snap to the guide. For the Snap to It feature to work, however, you need to make sure that it's turned on (and for more information about working with frames of all types, see Part 5, "Working with Frames").

✅ **Snapping to Ruler Guides**

You can also choose to have frames snap to the ruler guides you place on your pages. Choose **Tools, Snap to Ruler Marks**.

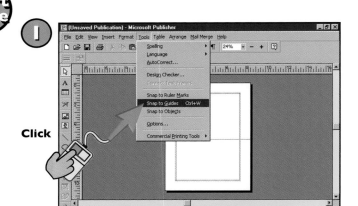

Start Here

Click

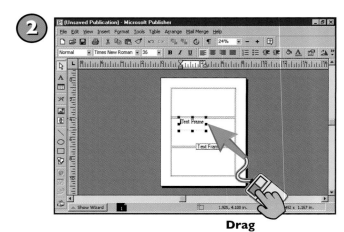

Drag

1 Choose **Tools**, **Snap to Guides**.

2 Drag the appropriate frame toward a grid guide on the page. When you release the frame, it snaps to the guide.

End Task

Task 10: Setting Page Margins

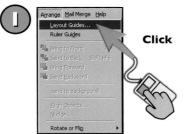

Click

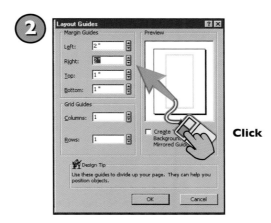

Click

Changing the Margins on a Page

When working with publication pages, you will want control over the page margins. This allows you to design how much white-space is between the page edges and your frames.

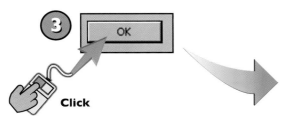

Click

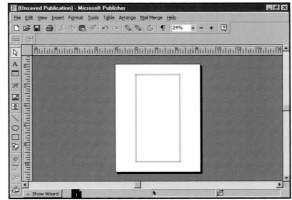

✓ **Move Your Margins with the Mouse**
You can also manually drag the margins on a page to a new location with the mouse. Choose **View, Go to Background** (discussed in the next task below). Then hold down the **Shift** key and drag any margin to a new location.

① Choose **Arrange**, **Layout Guides**.

② Click the appropriate arrows to increase (or decrease) the Left, Right, Top, or Bottom margin.

③ Click **OK**; the new margins appear on your page.

✓ **Type the Margin Increment**
When you are in the Layout Guides dialog box, you can type a new margin number in the appropriate margin box to quickly set that particular margin.

Task 11: Working in the Background

Getting to Know the Page Background

When you place various frames and other items on your page, you are working in the *foreground* of that page. If you want to place items that will be repeated on all the pages, such as page number, or the current date, you place them in the *background* of the page typically near the top or bottom margins. These items will then appear on each page of the publication. To place an item in the background, you must be in the Background view.

Your Frames Disappear

When you go to the background of a page, all the items you placed in the foreground seemingly disappear. Make sure that items you place in the background will not be obscured by objects in the foreground. The foreground basically overlays the background of the page.

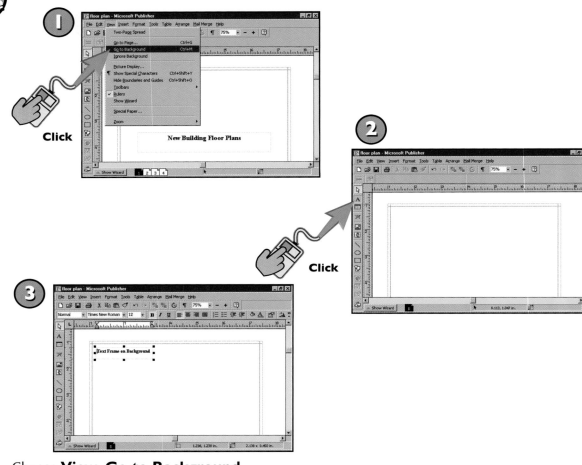

Start Here

Click

Click

1. Choose **View, Go to Background**.

2. Click a tool on the Publisher toolbar (for instance, the **Text Frame** tool), and draw a frame on the background.

3. Place text or other items in the frame that you want repeated on all the pages of the publication.

Task 12: Creating Headers and Footers

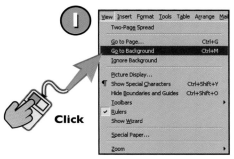

Click

Click

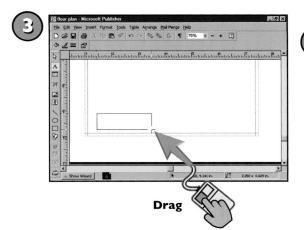

Drag

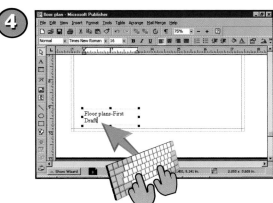

Placing Headers and Footers in the Background

If you need information to repeat on every page of a publication, you may want a *header* (an item repeating at the top of every page) or a *footer* (an item repeating at the bottom of every page). Once the header or footer are in place you can format the text (Part 3 describes working with text frames in the background or foreground of your pages).

① To place a header or footer in the publication, choose **View**, **Go to Background**.

② Click the **Text Frame** tool on the Publisher toolbar.

③ Hold down the left mouse button and drag to create a text frame either at the top or at bottom of the page (to create a header or footer).

④ Type the header or footer text in the text frame.

✓ Place Guides on the Background
If you don't want background items obscured by foreground frames, place guide lines on the background. These will appear on every page of the publication even when working in the foreground.

End Task

Task 13: Inserting Page Numbers

Creating Page Numbers in the Background

When you create publications that contain multiple pages, you may want to number the pages. Page numbers are placed in the background of the publication in a text frame. The great thing about using the page-number feature is that even if you insert or delete pages in the publication, the appropriate page number always appears on your pages because Publisher places a page-numbering code in the text frame. This code adjusts to page deletions or insertions, giving you the correct page number.

✅ **Adding Text to the Page-Number Frame**
If you want to have page numbers that read as "Page 1" (and so on), you can click just before the page number code (#) and add the text you want to appear on every page with the page number.

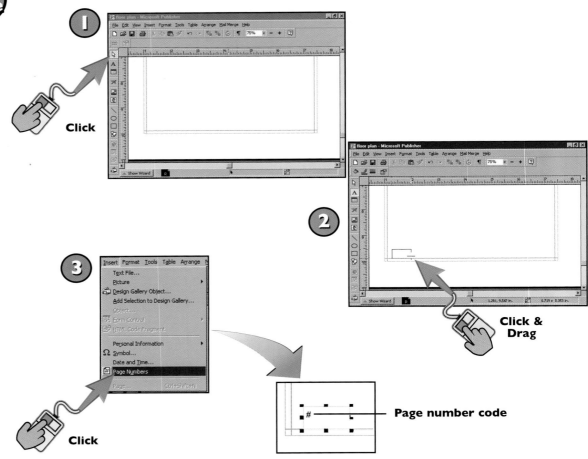

Start Here

Click

Click & Drag

Click

Page number code

1 In the background of a publication page, click the **Text Frame** tool on the Publisher toolbar.

2 Drag the mouse to create the text frame that will hold the page-number code.

3 Choose **Insert**, **Page Numbers**. A page-number code is placed in the text frame.

End Task

Task 14: Adding the Date

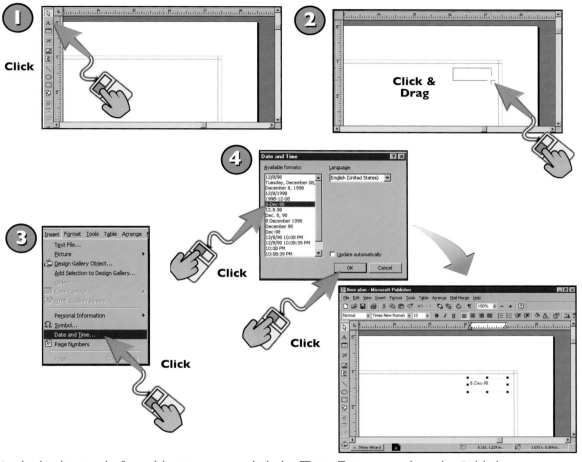

Click

Click & Drag

Click

Click

Click

Inserting the Date in a Text Frame

Another useful feature lets you automatically insert the date in a text frame. When you place this text frame in the background, you can conveniently place the current date on all the pages of your publication.

① In the background of a publication page, click the **Text Frame** tool on the Publisher toolbar.

② Drag the mouse to create the text frame that will hold the date-and-time code.

③ Choose **Insert**, **Date and Time**.

④ Choose the date format you want to place in the text frame, and then click **OK**.

✓ Updating the Date Automatically

If you want to have the date refreshed (to have the current date placed into the text frame that you placed the date code into), whenever you open the saved publication, click the **Update automatically** check box in the Date and Time dialog box.

Changing How Text Looks

How you format the text in your publication will help determine the overall look and feel of the publication pages. You can emphasize information by placing it in bold or a larger font size. You can add color to the page by placing text in a particular color. You will find that Publisher provides you with complete control over the look and formatting of text in a frame, such as the font style, font size, and color of your font.

Tasks

Task 1: Adding and Editing Text

Inserting a Text Frame on a Page

You add text to your publication in text frames by using the Text Frame tool on the Publisher toolbar. Because the text is contained in a frame, the width of the frame determines the length of the text lines in the frame.

Start Here

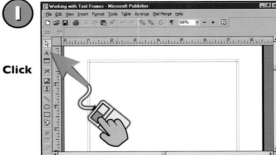

Click

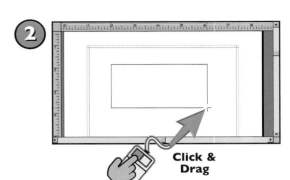

Click & Drag

Zooming In to Concentrate on Your Text

If you are in the Whole Page View when you place your text frames on your page, you may want to zoom in on the text before you type the text or attempt to edit it. Click the Zoom drop-down box on the Standard toolbar and select a zoom percentage that zooms you in on your page.

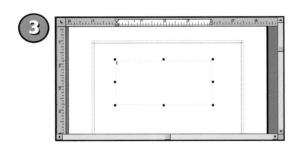

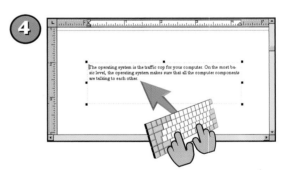

(1) Click the **Text Frame Tool** button on the Publisher toolbar.

(2) Click and drag to create the text frame on your publication page.

(3) Release the mouse button to end the frame-creation process.

(4) Type the text you want to place in the frame.

Next Step

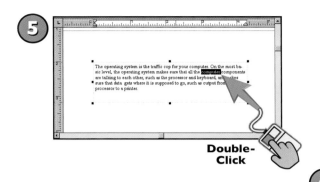

Double-Click

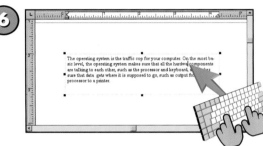

Editing and Deleting Text

You also can easily change and delete text in a text frame. It's just a matter of selecting the text you want to modify and then either typing new text or pressing the Delete key on the keyboard.

⑤ To change a word or line of text, either double-click on the word or drag to select the text.

⑥ Type the text that will replace the selected text.

⑦ To delete text, select the text to be deleted.

⑧ Press the **Delete** key.

✓ **Inserting New Text in a Text Frame**
Place the mouse pointer on the text in the text frame. The pointer becomes an I-beam. Click the I-beam on the text where you want to place the insertion point. Then type the text you want to insert into the text frame.

✓ **Different Ways to Select Text**
Double-click to select a word.

Drag to select a line or lines of text.

Triple-click to select all the text in the frame.

End
Task

Task 2: Cutting, Copying, and Pasting Text

Moving and Copying Text

You can also cut or copy selected text in a text frame and then paste it into another text frame or in another position in the current text frame. You use the same selection techniques discussed in the preceding task to select a word, a line or lines of text, or all the text in a text frame.

✓ **Pasting from One Page to Another**
You can also copy or cut text and then move to an entirely different page and paste the text into a new or an existing text frame.

✓ **Drag and Drop**
Another way to move text from one location to another is to drag and drop. Select the text to move and then drag it (a drag icon appears) to a new location. When you release the mouse button, you are "dropping" the text at the new location.

Start Here

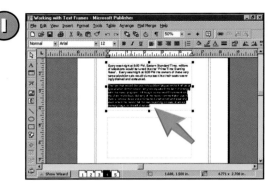

Click

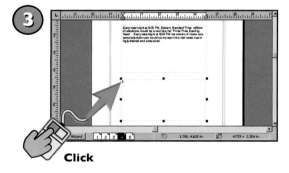
Click

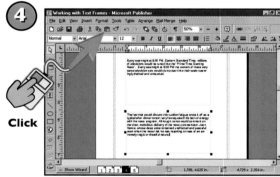
Click

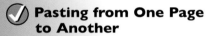

① Select the text you want to cut or copy (for example, drag to select a block of text).

② Click the **Cut** button or the **Copy** button on the Standard toolbar.

③ Place the I-beam where you want to insert the text, and click to place the insertion point.

④ Click the **Paste** button. The text is pasted at the insertion point.

End Task

Task 3: Choosing Fonts

Click

Click

Start Here

Changing the Font

The overall look of the text in a text frame is determined by the *font*. Fonts come in a wide variety of styles; the text you type in a new frame is created in the default Publisher font, which is Times New Roman, 10 point. You can easily change the font for new text or text that already exists in a text frame.

① Select the text in the text frame that you want to change the font for.

② Click the **Font** drop-down box on the Formatting toolbar, and choose a new font (such as **Rockwell**).

③ After changing the font, click outside the text frame to deselect it.

✓ **Typing New Text with a Different Font**
If you want to switch from the default font (Times New Roman) to a different font, select a new font from the Font drop-down box on the Formatting toolbar before you begin to type text in a brand-new text frame.

End Task

Task 4: Changing Font Size

Controlling Your Font's Size

You can change text font size in a text frame just like you change the font. Larger font sizes help you emphasize text. Increasing the font size also makes your text easier to read.

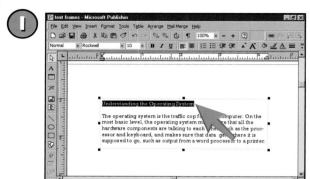

✓ **Font Size Is Measured in Points**

Font size is measured in points. A point is 1/72 of an inch, with the standard point size for business letters and other documents being 12 point. The higher the number of points (such as 18), the larger the font size.

✓ **Changing the Size of New Text**

Create a new text frame, and then select a new font size from the drop-down Font Size box before typing the new text.

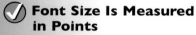

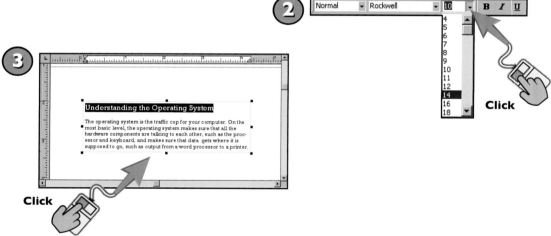

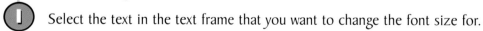

Click

Click

① Select the text in the text frame that you want to change the font size for.

② Click the **Font Size** drop-down box on the Formatting toolbar, and choose a new font size.

③ After choosing the new font size, click outside the text frame to deselect it.

Task 5: Formatting Characters

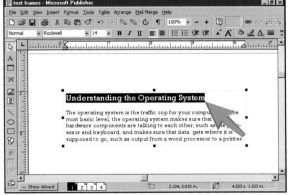

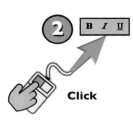

Click

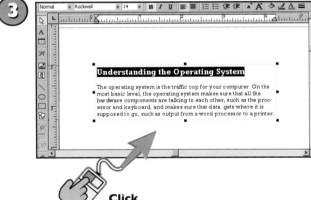

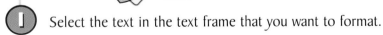

Click

(1) Select the text in the text frame that you want to format.

(2) Click the appropriate attribute button on the Formatting toolbar (**Bold**, **Italic**, or **Underline**).

(3) Click outside the text frame to deselect the formatted text.

Assigning Different Text Attributes

You also have control over various other font attributes associated with the text in your text frames. You can change the style of the font to bold, italic, or underline quickly. These font styles are readily available on the Formatting toolbar.

 Changing Other Text Attributes

You can also change font attributes for selected text in a frame by using the Font dialog box. Choose **Format, Font.** Use the Effects area check boxes to change the various font attributes (such as superscript, subscript, small caps, and so on).

End Task

Task 6: Changing Text Color

Emphasizing Text with Color

You can also change the color of the text in a text frame. Changing font color allows you to emphasize certain text and can add interest to your publication pages.

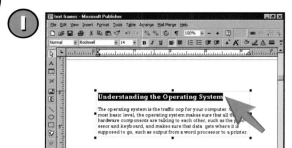

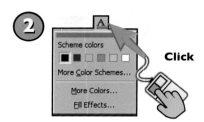

Click

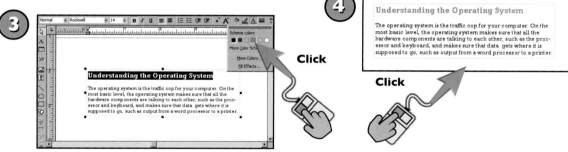

Click

Click

Click

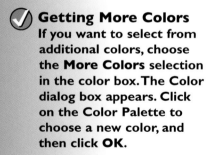

Getting More Colors
If you want to select from additional colors, choose the **More Colors** selection in the color box. The Color dialog box appears. Click on the Color Palette to choose a new color, and then click **OK**.

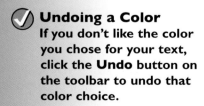

Undoing a Color
If you don't like the color you chose for your text, click the **Undo** button on the toolbar to undo that color choice.

1. Select the text in the text frame that you will change to a different font color.

2. Click the **Font Color** button on the Formatting toolbar.

3. Select a new color from the color box that appears (if you don't see a color you like, see the tip on this page).

4. Click outside the frame to deselect the text.

Task 7: Creating Drop Caps

 Start Here

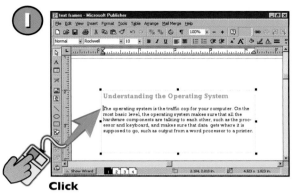

Click

Click

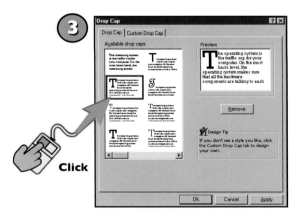

Click

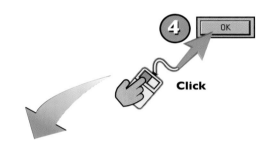

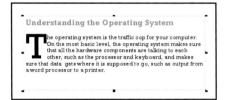

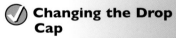

Click

Adding Flair to Text with Drop Caps

You can emphasize the beginning of a paragraph of text with a drop cap. A *drop cap* bolds and enlarges the first character of the first word in the paragraph, providing you with a nice design element to begin a text block.

✓ Changing the Drop Cap

After you assign a drop cap to text, you can easily change it to another drop cap style. Choose **Format, Change Drop Cap**, select a new style, and then click **OK**. You can also remove it by clicking **Remove** in the Drop Cap dialog box.

---

1 Click within a particular text line or paragraph in a text frame.

2 Choose **Format**, **Drop Cap**.

3 Choose a drop cap format in the Drop Cap dialog box.

4 Click **OK**. The drop cap appears in the paragraph.

 End Task

Task 8: Centering and Aligning Text

Changing Text Alignment

You have control over text alignment in the frames. You can center the text (in relation to the frame itself), right-align, left-align, fully justify the text, or use different alignments on different text lines or paragraphs in a text box.

✓ Working with Text Lines

You can have different lines in the same text frame aligned differently. For lines or paragraphs to be treated separately, all you have to do is place a line break (press Enter) between them.

✓ Aligning More Than One Paragraph at a Time

If you have a text box with more than one paragraph of information in it, you can select all or some of the paragraphs and then click an alignment button to change the alignment of several paragraphs at once.

Start Here

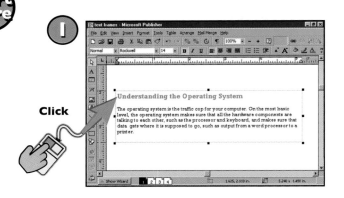

Click

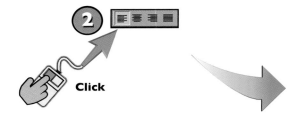

Click

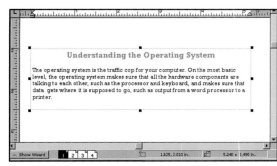

① Place the insertion point in the paragraph (any line or lines of text followed by a line break) you want to align.

② Click the appropriate button on the Formatting toolbar (such as **Center**, **Right**, or **Full**).

Task 9: Setting Indents

Start Here

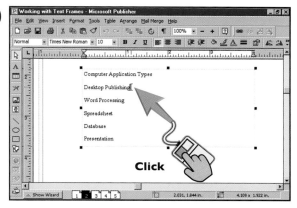

Click

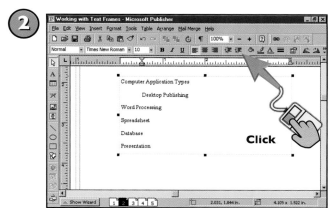

Click

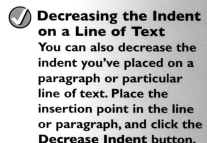

Indenting Text

You can offset text lines from other text in a text frame by using the indent buttons on the Formatting toolbar. Each time you click the Increase Indent button, your text is indented a half inch from the left edge of the text frame.

Decreasing the Indent on a Line of Text

You can also decrease the indent you've placed on a paragraph or particular line of text. Place the insertion point in the line or paragraph, and click the **Decrease Indent** button.

Indenting Several Lines of Text

To indent lines of text that are not part of the same paragraph (lines or blocks of text separated by a line return), select the lines and then click the **Increase Indent** button.

1 Place the insertion point in the text line or paragraph you want to indent.

2 Click the **Increase Indent** button on the Formatting toolbar.

End Task

Task 10: Setting Tabs

Using Tabs in a Publication

Another way to align text in a text frame is to use tabs. Tabs are set every half inch by default. Every time you press the Tab key on the keyboard, you offset the text line from the left margin of your text frame by one tab stop. To set tabs you click on the horizontal ruler to place a particular tab type on the ruler.

✓ Setting Different Tab Types

You can set different tab types by clicking on the tab selector (it appears where the two rulers join in the upper left).

Left Tab: Aligns the beginning of the text line at the tab stop.

Center Tab: Centers the text line at the tab stop.

Right Tab: Right-justifies the text line at the tab stop.

Decimal Tab: Lines up numerical entries at their decimal point.

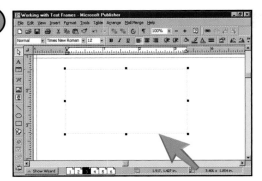

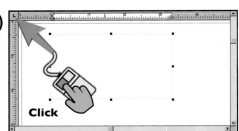
Click

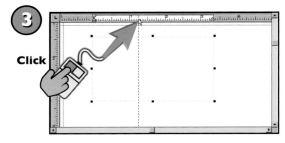
Click

1. Create a new text frame.

2. Click the tab selector to select the type of tab you want to place.

3. Click on the horizontal ruler at the position where you want to place the new tab.

4. Press the **Tab** key and type the text you want to align at the tab stop.

End Task

Task 11: Setting Line Spacing

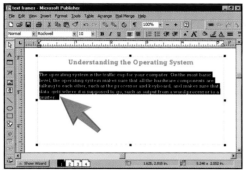

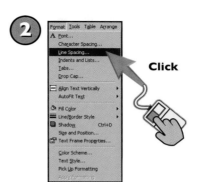

Click

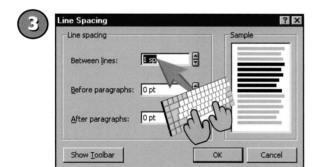

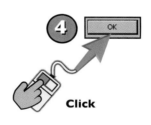

Click

Spacing Text in the Text Frame

Lines of text are automatically single-spaced, but, in some instances you may want to change the spacing. The text may be easier to read if double-spaced. You can easily change the spacing on text already existing in a text frame.

✓ **Setting Line Spacing Before Typing Text**
You can set new line spacing for a text frame, and then type the new text.

✓ **Setting Line Spacing Before and After Paragraphs**
The Line Spacing dialog box also enables you to add additional spacing before and after paragraphs that appear in a text frame. This makes it easy to offset paragraphs of information from each other or from other text elements.

① Select the text in an existing text frame that you want to change the line spacing for.

② Choose **Format**, **Line Spacing**.

③ Type in the new line spacing in the Between lines box (or click the arrows to select a new spacing).

④ Click **OK** to close the dialog box and apply the new line spacing.

Task 12: Creating Text Styles

Using Styles to Quickly Format Text

You can take several text attributes, such as the text size, color, and alignment, and save these attribute settings as a *style*. For instance, you may want to make text in certain text frames bold, italic, 12 point, and centered. Rather than assigning each attribute one at a time to the text, you can create a style that can do all the formatting at once by applying the text attributes to selected text.

✓ **Understanding Styles**
Styles can contain a mixture of formatting attributes. For instance, you might create a style that not only changes the color or size of text, but also changes its alignment, or automatically formats it as part of a list such as a bulleted list (for more about bulleted lists, see Task 15, "Creating Bulleted Lists," in this part).

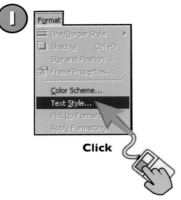

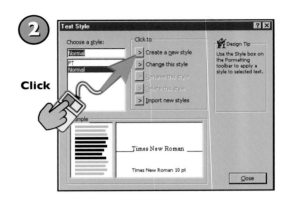

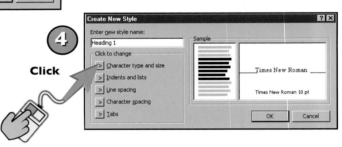

Click

1. Choose **Format**, **Text Style**.

2. Click the **Create a new style** button in the Text Style dialog box.

3. Type a name for the new style.

4. Click **Character type and size** in the Create New Style dialog box.

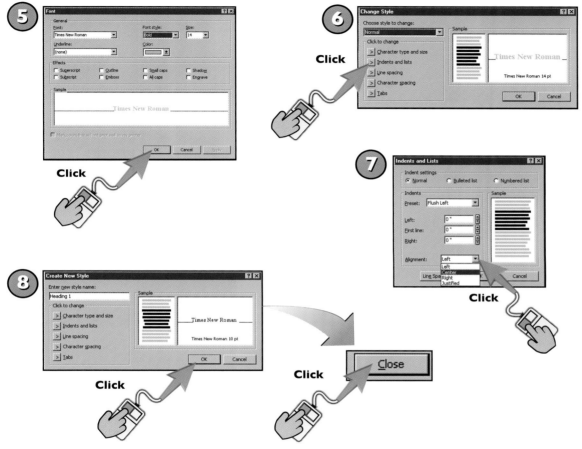

Using Styles for Consistency

Styles make it easy for you to keep the formatting of certain types of text items consistent. For instance, if you create a heading style with the appropriate character formatting (such as bold, italic, and a certain font size), you can assign this style to all your headings. This technique works great in situations in which you have two or three levels of headings in a publication. Create a style for each heading level and then assign it to text when needed.

(5) Choose the text formatting options you want to include in the style, and then click **OK**.

(6) Click **Indents and lists** in the Create New Style dialog box.

(7) Select the alignment options for the style, and then click **OK**.

(8) Click **OK** to close the Create New Style dialog box, and then click **Close**.

Task 13: Applying Styles

Assigning Styles to Text

After you've created your styles for a particular publication, you can assign those styles to text on the publication pages. Remember that styles allow you to assign several formatting attributes to the text at once by using a particular style.

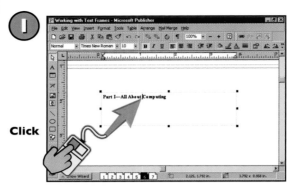

Click

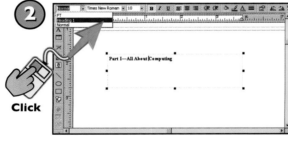

Click

✓ **Assigning Styles to More Than One Line**
If you want to assign a style to several text lines that are separated by line returns, select all the lines of text and then select a style from the Style box on the toolbar.

1 Place the insertion point in the line of text.

2 To assign the style to the text, click the **Style** drop-down box and select the appropriate style.

Task 14: Using the Format Painter

Start Here

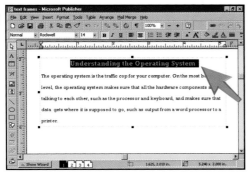

Click

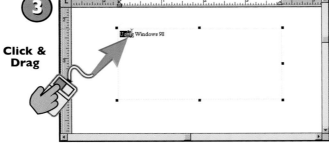

Click & Drag

Copying Text Formatting with the Format Painter

An alternative to creating styles is to use the Format Painter to copy the formatting attributes from already-formatted text and then apply the attributes to other text in your publication.

✓ **Applying Formatting to Multiple Text Entries**
You can apply copied formatting to more than one text entry with the Format Painter. Double-click on the **Format Painter** button and then apply the copied formatting to as many text lines as you want (on as many pages as you want). When you are done formatting, click the **Format Painter** button once to turn off the feature.

1 Select the text that has the formatting you want to copy.

2 Click the **Format Painter** button on the toolbar.

3 Drag the Format Painter icon across the text you want to apply the formatting to.

End Task

Task 15: Creating Bulleted Lists

Adding Bullets to Your Text Lists

You can quickly add bullets to a text list. Bullets help to delineate items in a list from other text in the text frame. You can add bullets to existing lists or turn on the bulleting and then type a new list.

Start Here

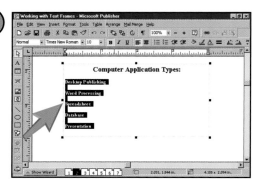

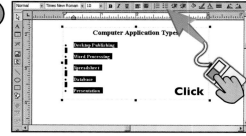
Click

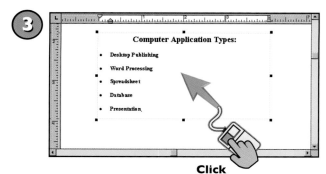
Click

Creating Bulleted Lists from Scratch

You can also create a bulleted list from new text. With the insertion point in a text frame, click the **Bullets** button on the toolbar. Then type the first bulleted item. Press **Enter** and then type the next bulleted item. Continue this process until you complete the list.

1 Select the text list you want to add bullets to.

2 Click the **Bullets** button on the toolbar.

3 Click anywhere to deselect the list.

End Task

Task 16: Creating Numbered Lists

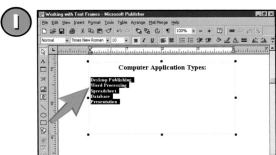

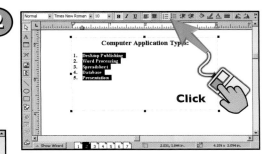

Click

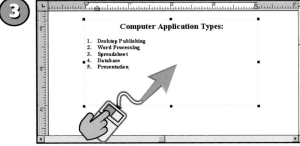

Click

Adding Numbers to Lists

You can also add numbering to a list of items in a text frame. The great thing about using Publisher's automatic numbering is that if you delete a line in the numbered list, all the numbering changes to accommodate the deletion.

Select the text list you want to number.

Click the **Numbering** button on the toolbar.

Click anywhere to deselect the list.

 Changing Number Styles

To change the number format for a list, select the numbered list and choose **Format, Indents and Lists.** Use the Format drop-down list to select a new numbering format for the selected list.

Task 17: Using WordArt

Creating Interesting Text Effects

When you want to add real interest to text elements in a publication, you can use WordArt. WordArt places a text object on your page that can be formatted with a number of eye-catching effects, such as text that wraps in a circle, text that curves, and text that flares out to the right or left.

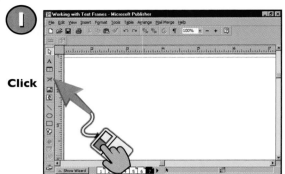

Click

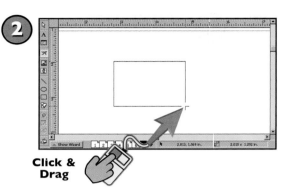

Click & Drag

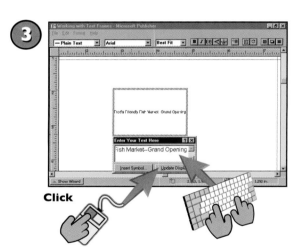

Click

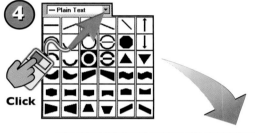

Click

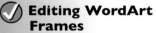

✓ Editing WordArt Frames

If you want to change the style of the text in the WordArt frame or change some other WordArt setting, double-click on the frame to access the WordArt toolbars and commands.

(1) Click the **WordArt Frame Tool** button on the Publisher toolbar.

(2) Drag to create a WordArt frame on the page.

(3) Type the text for the WordArt frame, and then click **Update Display**.

(4) Click the WordArt **Shape** drop-down box and select a style for the text; then click outside the WordArt frame to return to Publisher.

End Task

Task 18: Inserting Personal Information

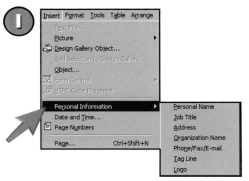

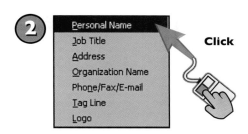

Click

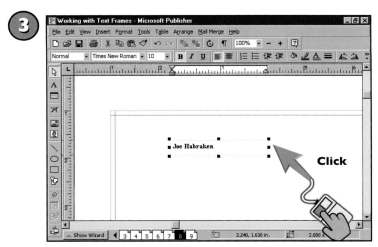

Click

Using Entries in Your Personal Information Profile

You can also quickly insert a new text frame into your publication that contains text that is taken from your personal information set. This allows you to place your name or other personal information into your publication quickly.

1. Choose **Insert**, **Personal Information**.

2. Choose the information you want to insert.

3. Click outside the new text frame to deselect it.

 Editing Your Personal Information Set
To edit your personal information set, choose **Edit, Personal Information**. Edit any of the information and then click **Update**.

Working with Pictures and Clip Art

Publisher provides you with a lot of flexibility in the types of objects you can add to your publication pages. You can add a picture file to a page, or you can choose to add a clip art image from the extensive clip art gallery that comes with Microsoft Publisher.

Tasks

Task 1: Inserting Pictures

Placing Pictures on Your Pages

Pictures can come in various file types, and they can consist of files you have on disk, items you copy from the World Wide Web, or pictures you create using a scanner or a digital camera (for more about inserting pictures from scanners and other sources, see Task 3, "Inserting an Image from a Scanner or Camera"). Inserting pictures can add interest to your publications.

Sizing the Picture Frame to Control Your Picture's Size
When you "draw" the picture frame on the publication page, its size determines the size of the picture that is inserted onto the page. If you want to fill a large space, create a large frame.

Click

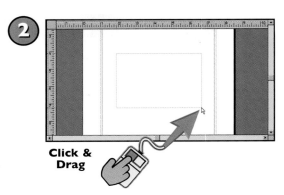

Click & Drag

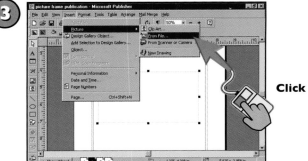

Click

① Click the **Picture Frame** tool on the Publisher toolbar.

② Place the mouse pointer on the page and drag to create the picture frame.

③ With the picture frame selected, choose the **Insert** menu and then point at **Picture**. Then choose **From File**.

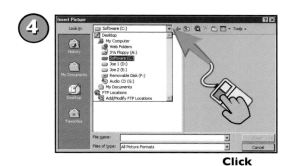

Double-Click

Click

Choosing the Right Picture File Format

Publisher can import many kinds of picture file formats. Some of the common file types it supports are Windows bitmaps (.bmp), CorelDraw files (.cdr), Joint Photographics Expert Group files (.jpg, used commonly on the Web), PC Paintbrush files (.pcx), and Window meta files (.wmf).

Click

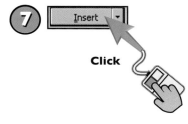
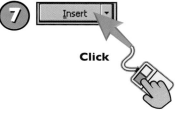

Click

4 In the Insert Picture dialog box, click the arrow on the **Look in** drop-down box to specify the drive where your file resides.

5 Double-click the folder that holds your file.

6 Choose the picture file.

7 Click the **Insert** button to insert the picture into your publication.

✅ **Opening the Insert Picture Dialog Box with a Double-Click**
You can also insert a picture file into a picture frame by double-clicking on the empty picture frame. The Insert Picture dialog box then appears.

End Task

Task 2: Inserting Clip Art

Using the Clip Art Gallery

Clip art is a library of ready-made images that are arranged in themes categories. The Publisher Clip Art Gallery is quite extensive.

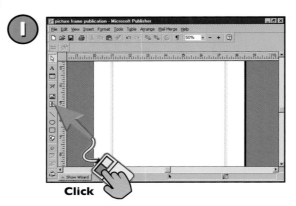

Click

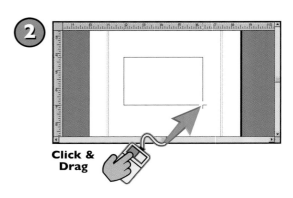

Click & Drag

✓ The Clip Art Gallery Offers More Than Pictures

The Clip Art Gallery has three categories marked as tabs: Pictures, Sounds, and Motion Clips. Yes, you can also insert sounds and motion clips into your publications (see Part 6, for more information about placing special objects on like these your pages).

Click

✓ Maximizing the Gallery Window

It's easier to view and navigate the Clip Art categories in if you maximize the Gallery window by clicking the Maximize button in the upper-right corner.

① Click the **Clip Gallery** tool on the Publisher toolbar.

② Place the mouse pointer on the page, and drag to create the clip art frame. The Insert Clip Art window appears.

③ Choose a category (such as **Animals**) to see the clip art available in that particular category.

Click

Click

Clip Art Size Is Related to Frame Size

When you first create the frame that will hold your clip art, make the frame the size you want the picture to be. The clip art will then fill its frame when you insert the actual clip.

Click

4 To insert a particular clip art image, click the image. A toolbar appears next to the image.

5 Click the **Insert clip** button, and the image is inserted into your publication.

6 When you have finished working with the Clip Art Gallery, click its **Close** (x) button to return to your publication.

Searching for Clips
You can also do a search for clip art by keywords. The clips that satisfy the search parameters will appear in the Gallery window. Click in the **Search for clips** box at the top of the Gallery window; type your search word and then press

End Task

Capturing Images Directly from a Device

You can also place images into your publications that come directly from a particular *input device*, such as a scanner or digital camera. You can have the scanner scan an image or the camera take a picture on-the-fly and then insert it into your publication.

✓ Selecting the Device You Want to Acquire the Image From

If you have more than one device attached to your computer for creating images, you can select the device you want to acquire the current image from. Choose the **Insert** menu and then point at **Picture**. Then choose **Select Device** on the cascading menu. In the Select Source dialog box that appears, choose the source device for the image, and then click **Select**.

Task 3: Inserting an Image from a Scanner or Camera

Start Here

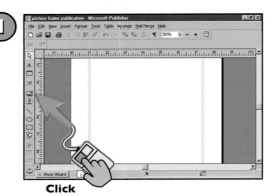

Click

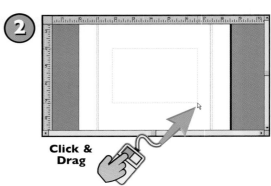

Click & Drag

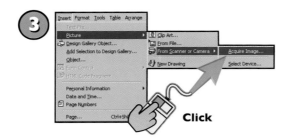

Click

Click

1. Click the **Picture Frame** tool on the Publisher toolbar.

2. Place the mouse pointer on the page, and drag to create the picture frame.

3. With the picture frame selected, choose the **Insert** menu and then point at **Picture**. Point at **From Scanner or Camera**, then point at **Acquire Image** on the cascading menu.

4. The image currently on your digital camera or on your scanner appears in the Capture dialog box; click **Capture** to place the image in the picture frame.

Task 4: Deleting Pictures

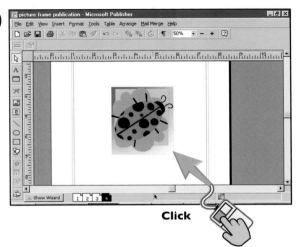

Click

Removing Unwanted Pictures

Removing pictures, clip art, and other images is really straightforward and requires only that you delete the frame that houses the particular image.

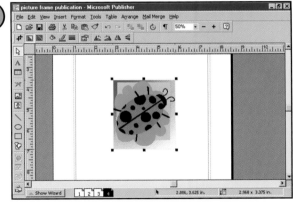

 Using Undo to Remove a Picture but Save the Frame
If you don't like a picture, but do like the frame, click the **Undo** button on the Standard toolbar. This removes the image but leaves the picture frame. You can then insert a different image into the frame.

 Click on the picture frame to select it.

 Press the **Delete** key on the keyboard.

 Replacing the Picture in the Frame with a New Picture
You can also select the picture frame and then use the Insert menu to insert either a new picture or a new clip art image.

Task 5: Resizing a Picture

Scaling Your Picture

You can easily size images using the mouse. Select the frame, then use the sizing handles that appear to change the image's size. To upscale an image, drag the image frame to enlarge it. To downscale an image, drag the frame to decrease its size.

Scaling Images with Percentages

Your overall image size is based on height and width. You can adjust either measurement by a percentage by using the Scale Picture dialog box. Choose **Format, Scale Picture.** The Scale Picture dialog box appears. Click in the **Scale height** box and enter a percentage for the image's height. Click in the **Scale width** box and enter a percentage for the image's width. Click **OK** when you've completed scaling the image.

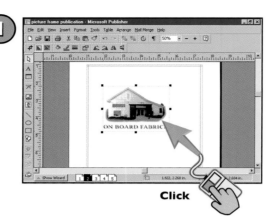

Click

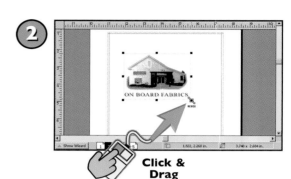

Click & Drag

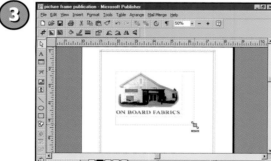

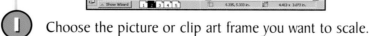

Choose the picture or clip art frame you want to scale.

Place the mouse pointer on any of the sizing handles that appear on the frame.

Drag to increase (or decrease) the size of the frame; this scales the picture inside the frame.

Task 6: Cropping a Picture

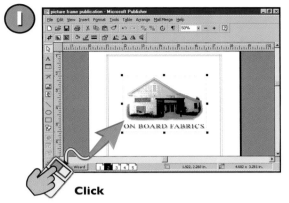

Click

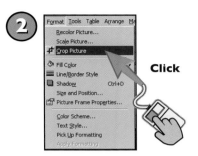

Click

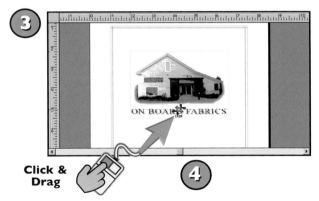

Click & Drag

(1) Select the picture or clip art frame that holds the image you want to crop.

(2) Choose **Format**, **Crop Picture**. The mouse pointer becomes a cropping tool.

(3) Place the cropping tool on any of the sizing handles on the picture's frame, and drag to crop the picture.

(4) Release the mouse and the picture is cropped.

Trimming an Image

You may run across a situation in which you would like to trim the edges off of a particular image. For instance, if you have a clip art image that contains a picture surrounded by a border, you may want to crop out the border and keep just the picture itself in the frame. Or you may have an image that contains several items, such as a picture of several people, and you might want to crop the image so that only one person appears in the frame. You can easily crop an image using the Publisher cropping tool.

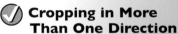 **Cropping in More Than One Direction**
After invoking the cropping tool, you can crop the image in more than one direction (such as on the right and then on the top) in the same cropping session. The cropping tool disappears only when you click outside the picture frame to deselect it.

Task 7: Changing Picture Colors

Recoloring an Image

You can change the color of an image in a picture or clip art frame to one selected color. This creates a monochrome: a picture made up of shades of one color. This special effect works best with images that were originally only one or two colors. You may have to experiement with different colors to find one that gives you gives you a satisfactory monochromatic image.

Start Here

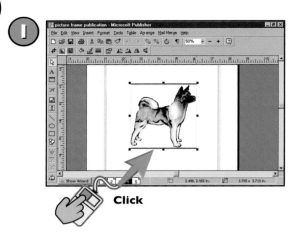

Click

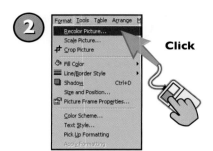

Click

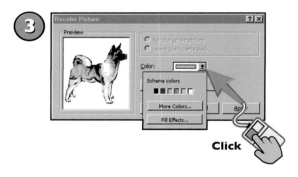

Click

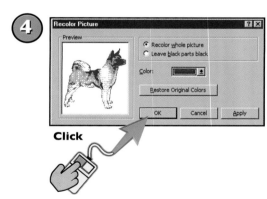

Click

✓ **Choosing More Colors**
If you want more colors than those in the Recolor Picture dialog box, click the **More Colors** selection. The Color dialog box appears. Choose any color on the palette, then click **OK** to return to the Recolor Picture dialog box.

① Select the frame that holds the picture or clip art you want to recolor.

② Choose **Format**, **Recolor Picture**. The Recolor Picture dialog box appears.

③ Click the arrow on the **Color** drop-down box to select a new color.

④ Click **OK** to close the dialog box and apply the new color to the image.

 End Task

Task 8: Pasting a Picture into a Publication

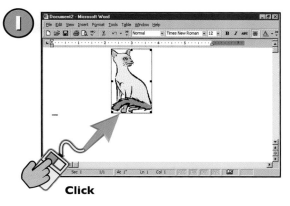

Click

Click

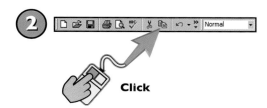

Click

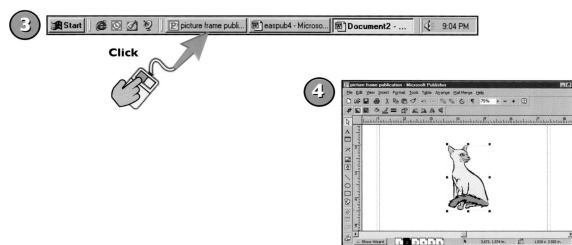

Inserting Pictures from Other Applications

You also can easily place pictures into Publisher from other Windows applications. For instance, you can copy a picture in Microsoft Word and then paste it into Publisher. Pasting pictures onto Publisher pages allows you to take advantage of images that you create in another application and want to immediately copy to your publication.

 Using Cut and Paste
You can also use Cut and Paste to move pictures from one page of a publication to another. For instance, you may want to move a picture from page one to page two. Select the image and then click **Cut** on the toolbar. Move to the page where you want to place the image, and click the **Paste** button.

1 Open the file and application that hold the image you want to copy, and then click on the image to select it.

2 Click the **Copy** button on the application's Standard toolbar (such as in Microsoft Word).

3 Click the **Publisher** application button on the Windows Taskbar to return to the Publisher window.

4 Click the **Paste** button on the Standard toolbar to paste the image onto your Publisher page.

Giving Your Picture a Caption

Although every picture does tell a story, in certain publications you may also want to include a picture caption that describes a picture. Rather than add a caption to your picture (which you can do with a simple text box), you may want to take advantage of the Publisher Design Gallery and some special picture frames it contains that are designed with an attached caption box.

✅ Adding a Text Box Caption

If you want to quickly add a caption to an existing picture, insert a new text frame below the picture and then add the caption text. Group the picture frame and the caption text frame. Then when you move the picture, the caption box will move with it.

Task 9: Adding Captions

Click

Click

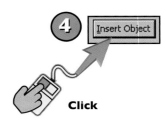

Click

① Click the **Design Gallery Object** button on the Publisher toolbar. The Design Gallery appears.

② Choose **Picture Captions** in the Categories pane of the Design Gallery.

③ Choose a particular picture-caption layout in the Picture Captions pane of the Design Gallery.

④ Click the **Insert Object** button to insert the picture-caption frame in the publication.

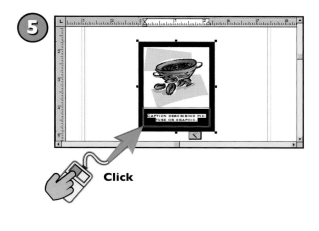

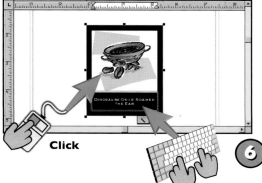

After you've placed the picture-caption frame onto the publication page, you still need to type your caption and insert the appropriate picture into the area of the caption frame that currently holds a picture placeholder.

Click

Click

Click

(5) Click in the caption area of the frame.

(6) Type the text for your picture caption.

(7) Click on the placeholder picture currently shown in the frame.

(8) Choose **Insert**, **Picture**. Choose **Clip Art**, **From File**, or **From Scanner or Camera** to replace the current placeholder picture.

✔ **Adding Other Special Elements to Your Publications**
You will find that the Design Gallery offers various other special design items you can add to your publication pages. It includes mastheads, which make great headings for your pages; sidebars, for placing notes and tips in a publication; and other special items such as calendars and coupons.

End Task

Task 10: Drawing with Microsoft Draw

Creating Your Own Pictures

You can also choose to draw your own images using Microsoft Draw. Microsoft Draw is an add-on application that comes with Publisher 2000 and Microsoft Office 2000. It provides an assortment of drawing tools you can use to create your own images. The tools available operate a great deal like the line, oval, and rectangle tools on the Publisher toolbar (these tools are discussed in Part 6).

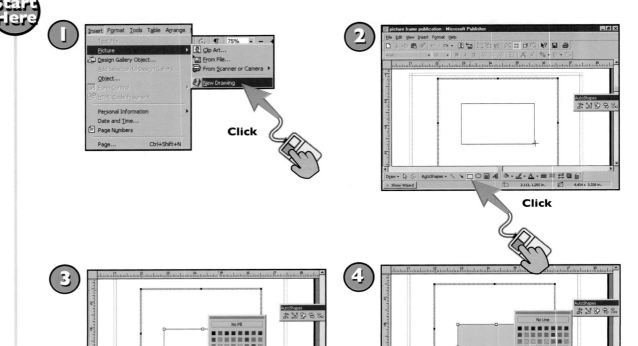

✓ **Draw Is Available in Other Microsoft Applications**
Microsoft Draw is a standard drawing tool available in all the applications that are part of the Microsoft Office 2000 suite.

1. Choose the **Insert** menu and then point at **Picture**. Then choose **New Drawing** on the cascading menu. The Draw toolbar appears.

2. Click a tool on the Draw toolbar (such as the rectangle), and drag to create an item in the draw frame.

3. With the drawn object selected, click the **Fill Color** button and choose a fill color.

4. With the object selected, click the **Line Color** button and choose a color to add a border.

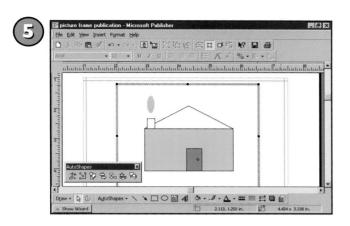

Draw Is a Separate Application

The difference between the Publisher drawing tools and Microsoft Draw is that the Publisher drawing tools create individual objects, whereas your Microsoft Draw image (made up of a number of drawn elements) is treated as a single object.

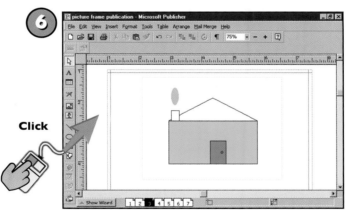

Click

Use other tools on the Drawing toolbar as needed to complete your drawing.

Click outside the draw frame to return to Publisher.

✓ **Understanding Draw**
When you start Microsoft Draw, the application actually takes over the Publisher window. You will notice that all the toolbars and commands normally found in the Publisher window are replaced by toolbars for Microsoft Draw. When you click outside the draw frame, you are returned to Publisher and its toolbars.

Working with Frames

When you place an item such as text, a picture, or another object on a publication page, you are actually inserting a *frame* that contains the item. Being able to insert, delete, or move frames and manage their border and color attributes enables you to give your publication pages a customized look and control the overall layout of individual pages.

Tasks

Task 1: Creating a Frame

Inserting a Frame on a Page

When you insert a frame on a page, you will actually insert a particular object onto that page such as text, a picture, or a drawn object. Once a frame is on the page, you can move the frame, change the layout of the frame, and format the item inside the frame.

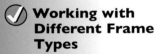

Start Here

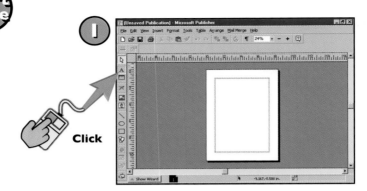

Click

✓ **Working with Different Frame Types**

After you create a new frame, your next action will depend on the type of frame you created. If you used the Text frame tool, you will type the text you want to place in a frame. If you used the Picture frame tool, you will insert some type of picture file.

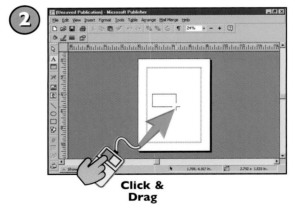

Click & Drag

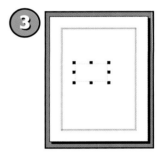

✓ **Undoing a New Frame**

If you place a frame on a page and want to quickly remove it, click the **Undo** button on the Standard toolbar.

1 Click a frame tool on the Publisher toolbar (such as the **Text** frame tool).

2 Click and drag to create the frame (you determine the height and width of the frame).

3 Release the mouse button to end the frame-creation process.

End Task

Task 2: Moving a Frame

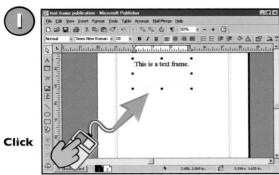

Click

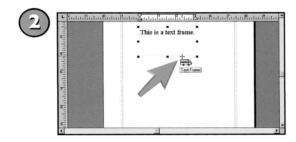

Selecting and Repositioning a Frame

Publisher also provides you with the ability to move your frames on your publication pages. You can drag any selected frame to a new position by using the mouse.

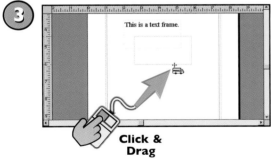

Click & Drag

① Click anywhere on a frame to select it.

② Place the mouse pointer on any of the border edges surrounding the frame (do not place the mouse pointer on the sizing handles). A Move pointer will appear.

③ Drag the frame to a new position on the page.

 Positioning the Frame Using Values

You can also place a frame on the page by using the Size and Position dialog box. Choose **Format, Size and Position** to open the dialog box. Use the **Horizontal Position** box to set the horizontal position for the frame, and use the **Vertical Position** box to set the vertical position. Click the **OK** button to finish.

Task 3: Nudging a Frame

Moving Frames with Precision

If you want to fine-tune the position of a frame in reference to other frames and objects on a page, use the Nudge feature. It allows you to move the selected frame a small distance in any direction. The Nudge feature gives you more precision than you get when dragging the frame with the mouse.

Start Here

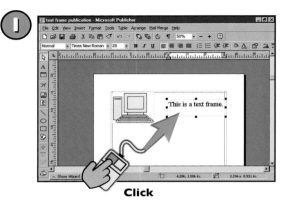
Click

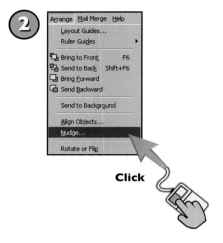
Click

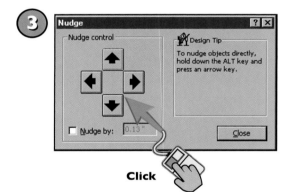
Click

✓ **Determining the Nudge Value**
To nudge the frame by a specific measurement, click the **Nudge by** check box and enter a number in the accompanying text box.

✓ **Using Guide Lines**
Another way you can position frames with more accuracy is to turn on the Snap to Guides feature (choose **Tools, Snap to Guides**). Frames then snap to the nearest grid line.

① Click anywhere on a frame to select it.

② Choose **Arrange**, **Nudge**. The Nudge dialog box appears.

③ Click the appropriate arrow button in the Nudge dialog box to nudge the frame in that direction.

End Task

Task 4: Deleting a Frame

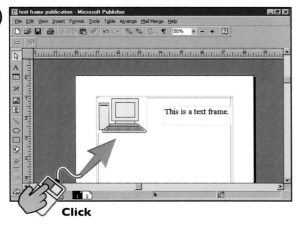

Click

Removing Unwanted Frames

As you build your publications, you will find that occasionally you create a frame (containing text or some other object) that you don't want on the page. You can easily delete frames from a publication page.

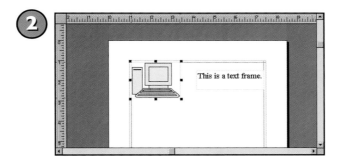

① Click on the frame to select it.

② Press the **Delete** key on the keyboard to remove the selected frame.

✓ **Cutting Instead of Deleting**
If you want to remove a frame from the current page and use it on another page in the publication, you can cut and then paste the selected frame. Select the frame and then click the **Cut** button on the toolbar. Move to the page you want to paste the frame on, and then click the **Paste** button on the toolbar.

Task 5: Copying a Frame

Making Multiple Copies of the Same Frame

You can also copy frames and place multiple occurrences of the same frame on a page, or copy a frame to another page in your publication. This allows you to easily place repeating design elements on a page or throughout an entire publication.

Start Here

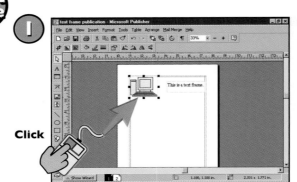

Click

Click

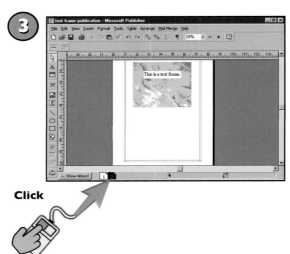

Click

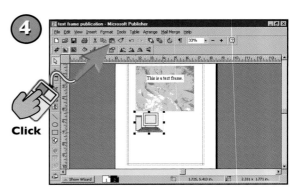

Click

✓ **Jumping to Whole Page View to Arrange Multiple Copies of a Frame**
You can quickly go to the Whole Page view by pressing **Ctrl+Shift+L** on the keyboard. This allows you to view the entire page as you arrange multiple copies of a particular frame.

1. Click on a frame to select it.

2. Click the **Copy** button on the Standard toolbar.

3. Select the page you want to place the copy of the frame on by clicking the Publisher page buttons on the status bar, or remain on the current page.

4. Click the **Paste** button to paste a copy of the frame onto the current page.

End Task

Task 6: Sizing a Frame

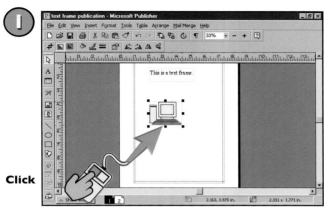

Click

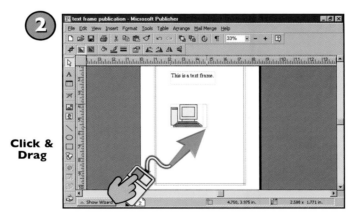

Click & Drag

Changing the Height and Width of a Frame

You can change the width or height of a frame on a publication page by using the sizing handles that appear on the selected frame.

✓ **Maintaining the Height/Width Ratio of a Frame**

To change the frame's size but maintain the current height-to-width ratio, place the mouse pointer on any diagonal sizing handle (positioned at a corner where the vertical and horizontal borders meet), and drag to change the overall size of the frame.

✓ **Typing Your Frame Settings**

You can also specify height and width measurements in the Size and Position dialog box. Choose **Format, Size and Position.** Set the frame the Height and Width boxes then click **OK.**

1. Click on a frame to select it.

2. Place the mouse pointer on any of the sizing handles, and drag the handle to change the width or height of the frame.

Task 7: Changing Frame Borders

Selecting Line Styles for Frame Borders

When you create a frame containing text or a picture (or other object), the frame itself is transparent and does not have a border (you see the border only when you select the frame). You can choose to place a border around the frame. You have control over the line weight and style of the lines that serve as the border around the frame.

✓ Formatting Selected Borders

You don't have to always place a box around a selected frame. You can select certain borders of the frame (such as the left vertical border or the bottom horizontal border) and add a border line to just this area of the frame. Open the Border Style dialog box (choose **Format, Line/Border Style, More Styles**). Use the Select a Side box to select certain sides of the frame for formatting.

Start Here

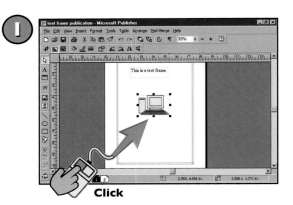

Click

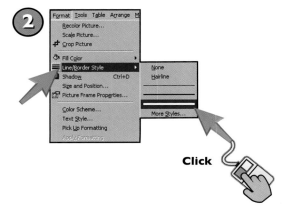

Click

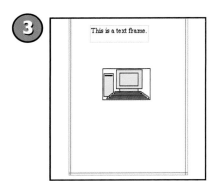

① Click on the frame you want to place the border around.

② Choose **Format**, **Line/Border Style**.

③ Choose a line style on the cascading menu that appears. A border appears around your frame.

Task 8: Applying Shading to Frames

Start Here

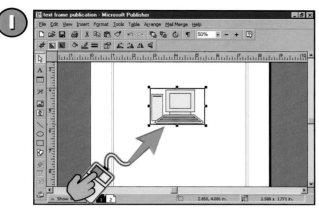

Click

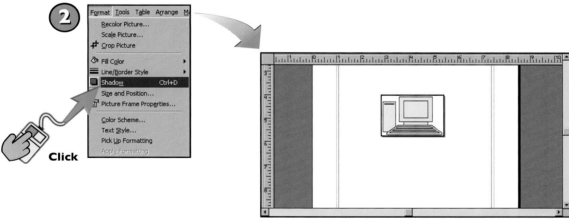

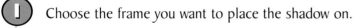

Click

Placing a Shadow on a Frame

You can also place a shadow on your frame border. This shading on the bottom and right sides of the frame add depth to the frame. Shadows particularly enhance the borders of text frames and picture frames. The shadow "lifts" the frame away from the publication page, giving it a 3D feel.

① Choose the frame you want to place the shadow on.

② Choose **Format**, **Shadow**. The shadow appears on the frame border.

 Shadows Work Best with Borders
You will find that shadows work best when a border has been placed around a frame. The shadow adds depth and definition to an otherwise flat border and frame.

End Task

Task 9: Working with Border Colors

Changing the Color of Frame Borders

To make your publication more eye-catching, you may want to change a frame's border color from default black to some other color by using the Border Style dialog box.

✓ **Choosing More Colors**
If you want more colors than provided by the Color drop-down box, click the **More Colors** button on the drop-down list. The Colors dialog box appears. Click on the **Color Spectrum** box to choose a new color for your frame borders, then click **OK**.

✓ **Using Colors on Selected Borders**
You can add color to selected frame borders. In the Border Style box, choose the **None** preset option to clear all previous line selections. Then click on the sides you want to add color to (a line will appear). Choose a color and click **OK** to close the dialog box.

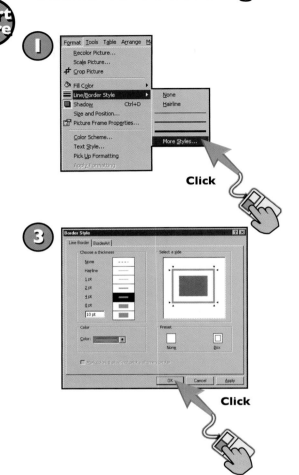

Click

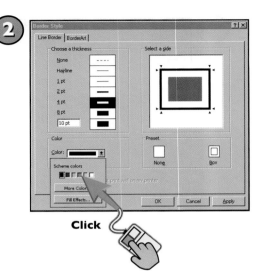

Click

Click

1. Choose **Format**, **Line/Border Style**, and then choose **More Styles** on the cascading menu to open the Border Style dialog box.

2. On the Line Border tab of the dialog box, click the **Color** drop-down box and choose a new color for the frame borders.

3. Click **OK** to close the dialog box and apply the new color to the frame border.

Task 10: Working with Frame Fills

Start Here

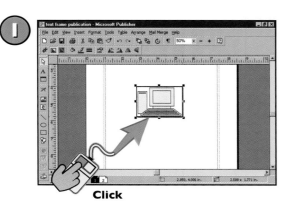
Click

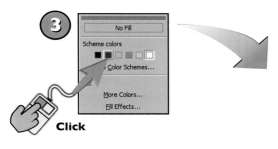
Click

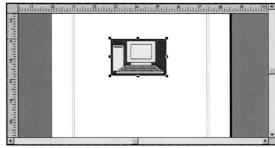

Placing Color Inside the Frame

A great way to add interest to your publications is filling a frame with a selected color. Be advised that when you do this, it can obscure the object residing inside the frame. For instance, you may have to change the text color so that it can still be read after putting a fill color in its frame.

✓ Using Fill Colors with Pictures

The fill color fills only the part of the frame (the interior) that is not occupied by the picture itself. The color, in effect, becomes a background for the picture.

✓ Selecting More Fill Colors

To access more fill colors, click the **More Colors** button on the cascading menu. In the Colors dialog box, click on the **Color Spectrum** box to select a new color for your frame borders, then click **OK**.

1 Choose the frame you want to add a fill color to.

2 Choose **Format**, **Fill Color**.

3 Choose a fill color from the cascading menu that appears. The fill color appears in the selected frame.

End Task

Task 11: Grouping Frames

Placing Frames in a Group

After you have frames placed on a page, you may want to adjust the overall positioning of all the frames in relation to the top or bottom of the page or some other special element on the page (such as a large banner heading). Moving each of the frames individually can be time-consuming and frustrating. The solution to this problem is to group the frames and then move them together as one unit.

Start Here

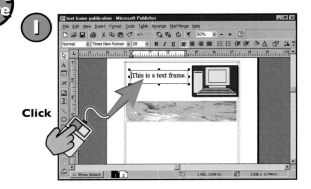

Click

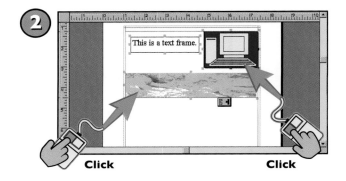

Click   Click

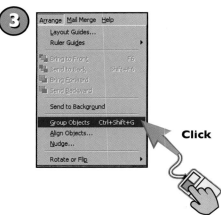

Click

✓ **Ungrouping Frames**
If you no longer want a series of frames in a group, choose **Arrange, Ungroup Objects.** The frames will now operate as separate frames rather than as part of a group.

① Select the first frame that will be in the group, by clicking on it.

② Hold down the **Shift** key and select additional frames. A selection box appears around all the selected frames.

③ To place the selected frames in a "permanent" group, choose **Arrange**, **Group Objects**.

End Task

Task 12: Wrapping Text Around Frames

Start Here

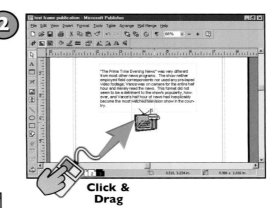

Click & Drag

Using Pictures and Text Together

If you want to have a block of text wrap around a picture or object, you need to create both a text frame and a picture frame. You can then place the picture frame on top of the text frame. The text will wrap around the picture frame, providing a nice visual effect for your publication page.

Wrapping the Text Around the Frame or Around the Picture
You can wrap the text around the picture frame or around the picture inside of the frame. To choose, just select the frame; then choose **Format, Picture Frame Properties**. In the Picture Frame Properties dialog box, click either the **Entire Frame** or the **Picture Only** radio button.

① Create a text frame and a picture or clip art frame on the publication page (see Task 1, "Creating a Frame," in this part for more help in creating a frame).

② Drag the picture or clip art frame onto the text frame.

③ Position the picture or clip art frame so that the text in the text frame wraps to your liking.

End Task

PART 6

Adding and Formatting Objects

An *object* is any item you add to your publication pages. Objects can be pictures or text frames, or they can be special objects such as logos, calendars, and coupons. Publisher provides a set of Wizards in the Design Gallery that create *smart objects* (such as logos, mastheads, and other special objects) that you can edit at any time by invoking the appropriate Wizard. Publisher also provides a set of drawing tools you can use to create your own objects. And if that's not enough, you can copy and paste items from any number of other applications such as Microsoft Word or Microsoft Excel to add special **OLE** (*Object Linking and Embedding*) objects to your publications.

Tasks

Creating Smart Objects

When you insert a smart object using the Design Gallery, you can easily edit the object using a Wizard specific to the object you selected. Using Design Gallery objects adds eye-catching elements to your publications.

✓ **Dealing with Oversized Objects**
Some of the smart objects created with the Design Gallery cannot be accommodated by a typical page size. You will have to size the new object to fit within the boundaries of your page.

✓ **Undoing a New Object**
If you place an object on a page and want to quickly remove it, click the Undo button on the Standard toolbar.

Task 1: Using the Design Gallery

Click

Click

Click

Click

1. Click the **Design Gallery Object** tool on the Publisher toolbar.

2. In the Design Gallery window, choose an Object category in the Categories pane.

3. In the Object pane (which shows all the objects in a particular category, such as Calendar), click the object you want to insert on the page.

4. Click the **Insert Object** button to insert the object onto the page.

Task 2: Editing a Smart Object

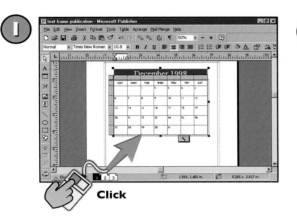

Click

Click

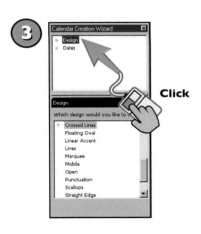

Click

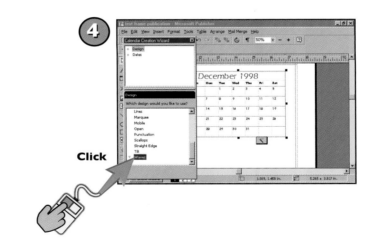

Click

Changing the Look of a Smart Object

When you add smart objects to your publication using the Design Gallery, Publisher makes it very easy for you to change the formatting of any of these special items. A Wizard is associated with each of the smart objects, and you can consult that Wizard to make changes to a particular object.

✓ Closing the Smart Object Wizard

When you have finished working with the Wizard for a smart object, you can close the Wizard to give yourself more working room in the Publisher window. Click the **Close** button in the upper-right corner of the Wizard window.

---

① Click on the smart object to select it.

② Click the **Wizard** button that appears on the smart object's border.

③ Choose the Design category (or any other category of attributes found in the top pane of the specific Wizard window).

④ Click a new design setting in the list found in the lower pane of the Wizard. The new design settings are applied to the selected object.

Task 3: Inserting Drawn Objects

Drawing Your Own Objects

Although you can insert many kinds of objects using the Design Gallery or objects created in other applications (see Task 14, "Inserting Objects from Other Applications"), you can also draw your own objects. Publisher provides you with drawing tools that make it easy to draw circles, rectangles, and lines. Drawn objects are the same as any other objects you insert into your publications. You can change their fill colors, resize them, and move them on the page.

✅ Getting Your Dragging Technique Down

When creating a new drawing object such as a circle or rectangle, drag the mouse downward on the page to create the height for the object, and then drag to the right to create the width for the object. This gives you greater control over the final size of the object.

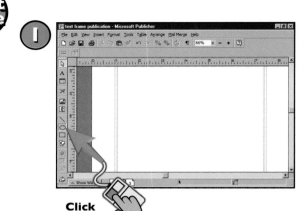

Click

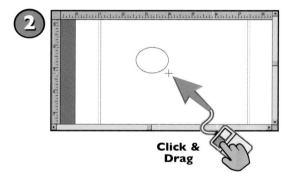

Click & Drag

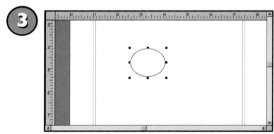

1. Click one of the Drawing tools on the Publisher toolbar (such as the **Oval** tool).

2. Drag on the publication page to create the drawn object (such as a circle).

3. Release the mouse button and your new drawn object appears on the page.

End Task

Task 4: Resizing Objects

Start Here

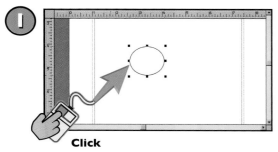

Click

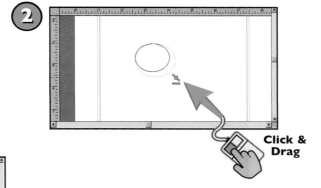

Click & Drag

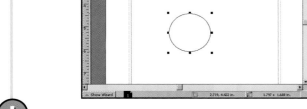

Changing the Size of Objects

Whether you draw your objects or create objects using the **Design Gallery**, you can change the size of any object using its sizing handles. Sizing objects is very similar to sizing text and picture frames (see Task 6, "Sizing a Frame," in Part 5, "Working with Frames"); you size objects by using the mouse.

(1) Click on the object you want to resize to select it.

(2) Place the mouse pointer on any of the sizing handles on the object, and drag to increase the object's size.

(3) Release the mouse button after you have attained the appropriate new size for the object.

 Drawing a Perfect Circle or Square
If you want to draw a perfect circle or square using the **Oval** or **Rectangle** tool, hold down the **Shift** key as you drag to create your new object.

End Task

Task 5: Moving an Object

Placing Your Objects on the Page

You can drag any of the objects you create to any position on your page.

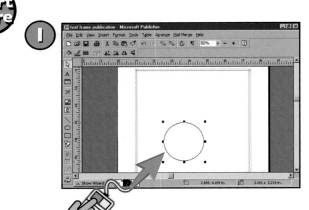

Click

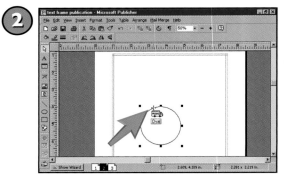

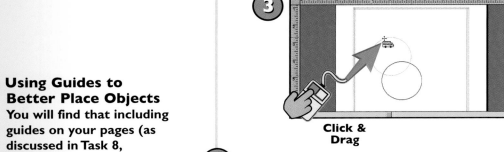

Click & Drag

✅ **Using Guides to Better Place Objects**

You will find that including guides on your pages (as discussed in Task 8, "Setting Ruler and Grid Guides," of Part 2, "Managing Publications and Working with Pages") provides additional help in placing objects in such a way that your publication shows good design sense.

1 Click on an object to select it.

2 Place the mouse pointer on the edge of the object so that the Move pointer appears.

3 Drag the object to a new location on the page.

Task 6: Centering Objects

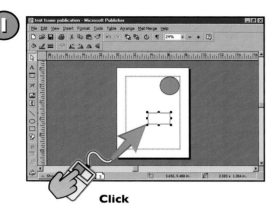

Click

Click

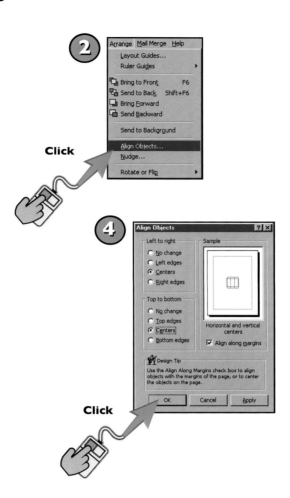

Placing Objects in the Center of a Page

You may drag an object to center it on a page. However, you will find that you can accurately center any selected object (or objects) on the page by using the Align Objects dialog box.

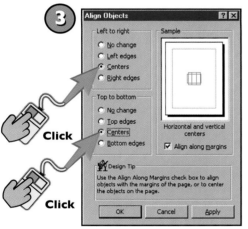

Click

Click

Click

✓ **Aligning Objects on the Edge of the Page**
The Align Objects dialog box also makes it easy for you to align objects at the top, bottom, left, or right edges of a page. Click the appropriate radio button in the dialog box.

✓ **Selecting Multiple Objects**
If you want to quickly align several objects using the Align Objects dialog box, click to select the first object and then hold down the **Shift** key and click on subsequent objects to select them. Then choose **Arrange, Align Objects** to open the **Align Objects** dialog box.

1. Click on an object to select it.

2. Choose **Arrange**, **Align Objects**.

3. In the Align Objects dialog box, click the **Centers** radio button in either the Left to right or the Top to bottom box to center the object accordingly (or click both).

4. Click **OK** to close the dialog box.

Task 7: Rotating and Flipping Objects

Rotating an Object

You can easily rotate objects you create on your publication pages. Rotating an object allows you to reorient the object to the right or the left. For instance, if you want to make a horizontal line into a vertical line, you can rotate the line to the right.

Start Here

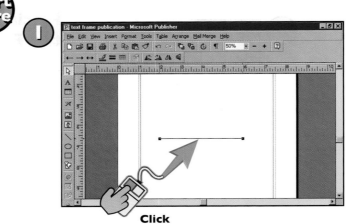

Click

✓ **Using Custom Rotation**
The Rotate Right and Rotate Left commands rotate an object 90 degrees in either the right or the left direction. If you want to custom-rotate an object, select the object and then click the **Custom Rotate** button on the Formatting toolbar. In the Custom Rotate dialog box that appears, click either the **Rotate Left** or the **Rotate Right** button to increase the rotation angle in that direction.

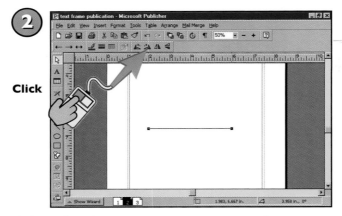

Click

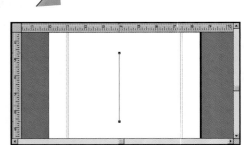

1 Click on the object you want to rotate to select it.

2 Click the **Rotate Right** (or **Rotate Left**) button to rotate the object in that direction. The object rotates.

Flipping an Object

You can also change the orientation of an object by flipping it. For instance, you may have a right-pointing object (such as a clip art arrow) that you would like to orient so that it points to the left. You can flip the image to the left to get a mirror image of the original image.

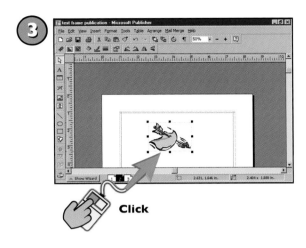

Click

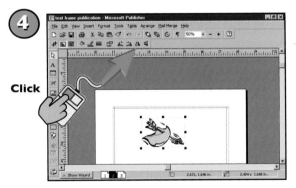

Click

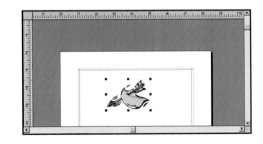

3 Click on the object you want to flip to select it.

4 Click the **Flip Horizontal** button to reverse the orientation of the object on the horizontal (or click the Flip Vertical to flip the object on the vertical).

⚠ Warning
A symmetrical object such as a circle or a square will look exactly the same no matter how many times you flip it from left to right or top to bottom.

Task 8: Setting Object Border Colors

Changing the Color of Drawn Object Borders

You can change the outside line or *border* color on drawn objects. This allows you to take advantage of color as a design element if you are going to print your publication using a color printer.

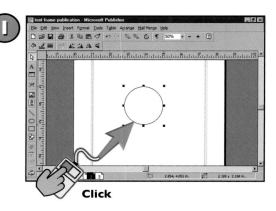

Click

✅ **Changing the Border Line Weight**
Click the **Line/Border Style** button on the Formatting toolbar to change the line weight (thickness) for the selected object.

✅ **Getting More Colors**
Click the **More Colors** button on the color palette to choose additional colors in the Colors dialog box.

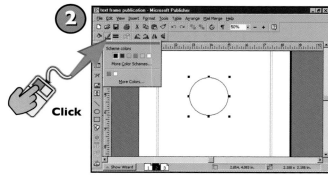

Click

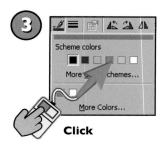

Click

1 Click on the drawn object that you want to change the line color for, to select it.

2 Click the **Line Color** button on the Formatting toolbar.

3 Choose a color on the color palette that appears.

Task 9: Setting Object Fill Colors

Start Here

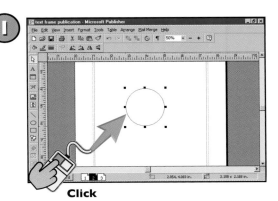
Click

Placing Color Inside an Object

You can also add color to the interior of drawn objects. The color adds visual interest and can also highlight a particular portion or set of objects on the page. Using fill colors and border colors on your objects can help you create objects with real impact.

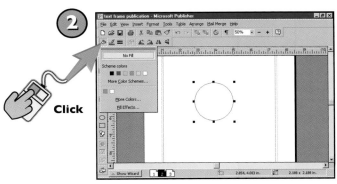
Click

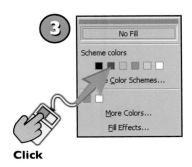
Click

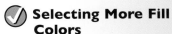

① Selecting More Fill Colors

If you want to choose from more colors than are provided by the **Fill Color** menu, click the **More Colors** button on the Color palette. The Colors dialog box appears. Click on a color box to select a new color for your object border. Then click **OK** to close the dialog box.

① Choose the object you want to select a fill color for.

② Click the **Fill Color** button on the Formatting toolbar.

③ Choose a Fill Color on the Color palette that appears.

End Task

Task 10: Layering Objects

Stacking Objects in Layers

You may find occasion to layer several objects on top of each other in a stack. For instance, you may want to place a circle on top of a square to create a design element. You can layer multiple objects by using the layering commands on the Standard toolbar or the Arrange menu.

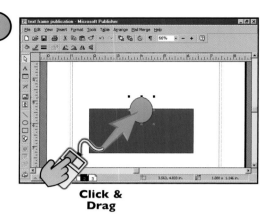

Click & Drag

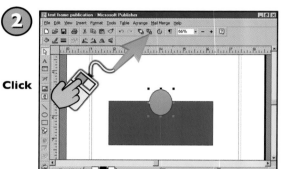

Click

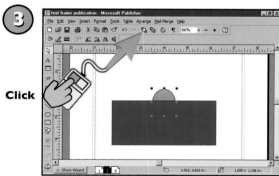

Click

✓ **Working with Stacks of Several Objects**
You can work with several stacked objects and easily place them in the stack by using the Arrange menu commands. You can move an object up one position in a stack by choosing the **Bring Forward** command. To move an object down one layer in a stack, choose the **Send Backward** command.

1 Drag an object (such as a circle) onto another object (such as a drawn rectangle).

2 To send the top object to the bottom of the current object stack, click the **Send to Back** button on the Standard toolbar.

3 To bring a selected object to the front of the stack, click the **Bring to Front** button on the Standard toolbar.

Task 11: Grouping Objects

Start Here

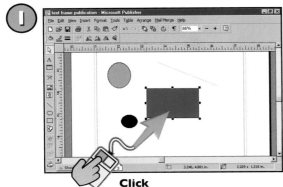

Click

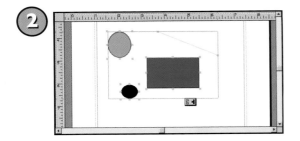

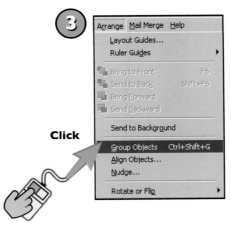

Click

Creating Object Groups

You can select a number of objects and make them part of a group. You can then move this group of objects as if it were one object, or you can select the fill color or border color for all the objects in the group.

✓ Formatting Object Groups

After you've placed several objects in a group, you can quickly format the fill color or the border color for the group. Click either the **Fill Color** or the **Line Color** button on the Formatting toolbar, and select a color.

✓ Ungrouping Groups

You will find that whenever you click on an object that's a member of a group, all the objects in the group become selected. To break a group, select the group and then choose **Arrange, Ungroup Objects**.

1. Select the first object that will be in the group, by clicking on it.

2. Hold down the **Shift** key and select additional objects. A selection box appears around all the selected objects.

3. To group the objects, choose **Arrange, Group Objects**.

End Task

Task 12: Using Snap to Objects

Using Objects as Guides for Other Objects

Using guides to help you align objects on your pages was discussed in Task 8 of Part 2. You can also use objects to help you align other objects. You do so by turning on the *Snap to Object* feature. Then when you drag an object near an already-placed object, the object being moved snaps to the static object.

Start Here

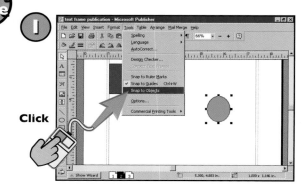

Click

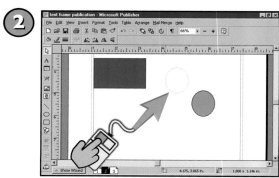

Click & Drag

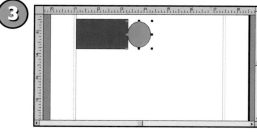

✓ Turning Off Snap to Objects

If you find that you would rather use grid lines or some other method to place your objects, choose **Tools, Snap to Objects** to remove the check mark next to the Snap to Objects feature. This turns off the feature.

1 Choose **Tools**, **Snap to Objects**.

2 Drag an object toward another object on the page.

3 Release the dragged object near the edge of the stationary object, and the released object snaps to the side of the stationary object.

End Task

Task 13: Inserting Video or Sound Objects

Start Here

Click

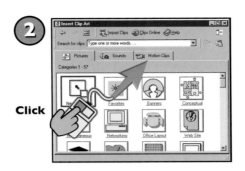
Click

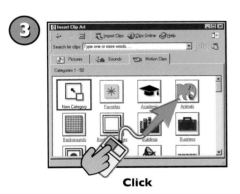
Click

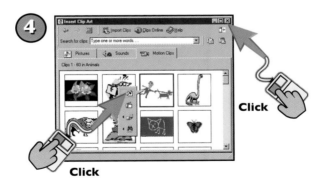
Click

Placing Video and Sound in Publications

If you are creating a publication that will be viewed on your computer or online (such as a Web site; see Part 9, "Using Advanced Publisher Features and Creating a Web Page," for information on using Publisher to build a Web site), you can add video and sound to the publication. This capability enables you to add some very interesting visual and sound effects to any presentation. You can find both of these media types in Publisher's Clip Art Gallery.

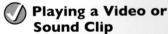
Playing a Video or Sound Clip
If you want to play a video or sound clip before you place it in your publication, choose the video or sound clip in the Clip Art Gallery, and then click **Play Video** or **Play Sound** on the toolbar that appears.

---

1 To insert an audio or video clip into a presentation, choose **Insert**, **Picture**, **Clip Art**.

2 In the Clip Art window, choose the **Sounds** or **Motion Clips** tab.

3 Choose a category of sounds or videos (such as **Animals** on the Motion Clips tab) from the selected tab (the categories available will depend on the tab you selected).

4 Choose a sound or video in the window and click the Insert button to place it on the publication page. Click the **Close** button.

End Task

Task 14: Inserting Objects from Other Applications

Using Objects Created in Other Applications

You can also place objects created in other applications into your publication. For instance, you can place an Excel worksheet and a chart into a publication. Or you can place a PowerPoint slide on a publication page. These types of objects are often referred to as Object Linking and Embedding (OLE) objects.

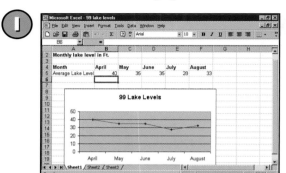

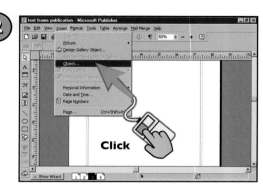

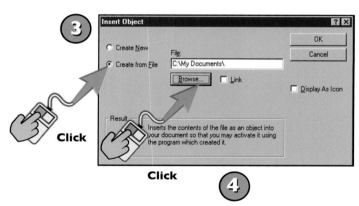

Create an object in any Windows application, such as a worksheet and chart in Microsoft Excel. Save the workbook as a file.

In Publisher, choose **Insert**, **Object**.

In the Insert Object dialog box, click the **Create from File** radio button.

Click the **Browse** button to open the Browse dialog box.

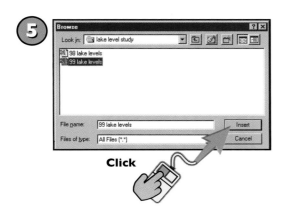

Click

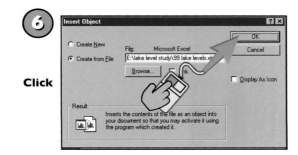

Click

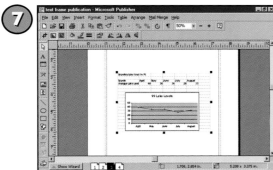

Working with OLE Objects

When you place **OLE** objects on your publication pages, you can actually edit them using the features of the application you created them in (such as **Excel**). Double-clicking on an **OLE** object in **Publisher** changes the **Publisher** menu system and toolbars to provide the features that are available in the *server application* (the application where the object was created).

 **Working with Other Embedded Objects**

An object you create using the **WordArt** tool in **Publisher** is another example of an **OLE** embedded object. You can edit a **WordArt** object by double-clicking on the object itself (double-click on any **OLE** object to edit the object).

⑤ Click the file you want to insert as the OLE object.

⑥ Click the **Insert** button in the Browse dialog box. You are returned to the Insert Object dialog box.

⑦ Click **OK** to close the Insert Object dialog box. The object is placed on your publication page.

Working with Tables

Another way to present information in a publication is to use a table. A table allows you to place information into rows and columns, making it very easy to arrange information in a highly accessible format. The intersection of a row and column is called a **cell**. And the cells are where you will place your data. Publisher gives you complete control over the number of rows and columns in your table and their size.

Tasks

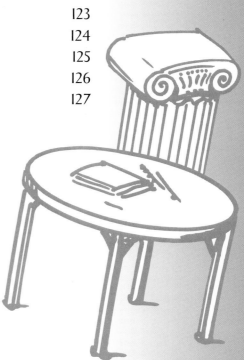

Task 1: Creating a Table

Inserting a Table on a Page

Tables are added to a publication page much the same as any object (such as a text frame or picture frame). You use the Table tool on the Publisher toolbar.

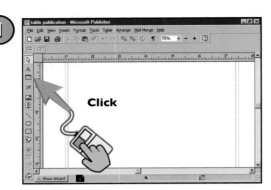

Click

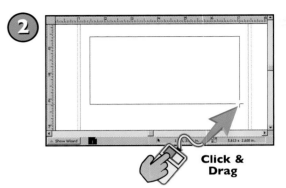

Click & Drag

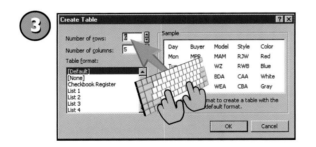

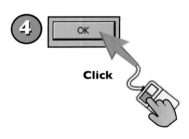

Click

Tables Are Great for Placing Information in Columns

When you want to place information side-by-side on the page, you will find that tables make this a simple task. Using tables gives you much more control over the placement of information than trying to align items with indents or tabs.

(1) Click the **Table** tool on the Publisher toolbar.

(2) Click and drag to create the table on the page.

(3) In the Create Table dialog box, type the number of rows and columns for the table.

(4) Click **OK**.

Task 2: Moving a Table

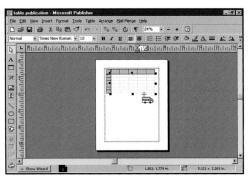

Placing Your Table on the Page

Tables are contained in a frame, just like the other objects you've worked with in Publisher. You can drag the table to a new location at any time.

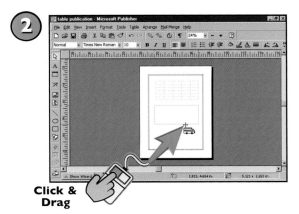

Click & Drag

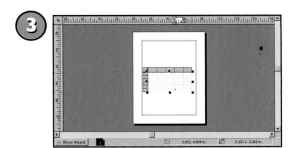

 Pasting from One Page to Another

You can also copy or cut the table and then paste it on a different page in the publication.

1 With the table selected, place the mouse pointer on the edge of the table frame.

2 When the Move icon appears, drag the table to a new location.

3 Release the mouse button when the table is in the correct position.

 End Task

Task 3: Resizing a Table

Changing the Table Size

You can resize a table at any time. When you change the table's width (make it larger or smaller), the change also affects all the column widths. If you change the table's height, this changes all the row heights in the table.

Start Here

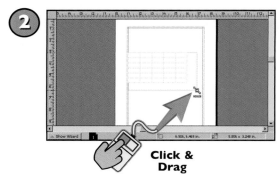

Click

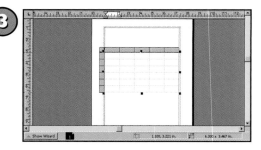

Click & Drag

✓ Maintaining the Table's Height/Width Ratio

If you want to maintain the table's overall height/width ratio when you increase or decrease the size of the table, be sure to drag one of the table's corners on the diagonal.

1 Click on the table to select it.

2 Place the mouse on the appropriate sizing handle, and drag to increase or decrease the size.

3 Release the mouse button.

Task 4: Resizing Table Columns

 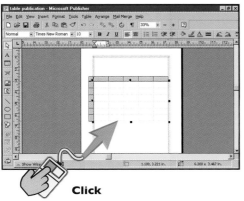

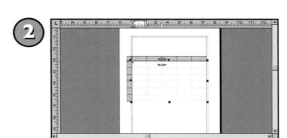

Click

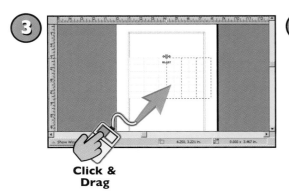

Click & Drag

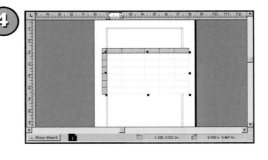

Controlling Column Widths

You've already seen that when you change the width of a table, the relative widths of all the columns in the table also change. You can also control the individual width of each column in the table to better accommodate text entries you place in a particular column.

 Keeping the Table's Size the Same When Widening Columns
When you increase individual column widths in a table, you might make the table wider than the page that the table is on. If you hold down the **Shift** key while dragging the column width tool, the table stays the same size and only the columns are widened.

(1) Click on the table to select it.

(2) Place the mouse pointer on a column divider to the right of the column you want to size.

(3) Drag to increase or decrease the width of the column.

(4) Release the mouse button.

Task 5: Resizing Table Rows

Changing Row Heights

You also have control over the height of the rows in the table. You change them much the same way as you did the width of a column.

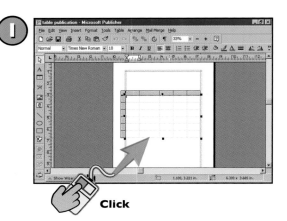

Click

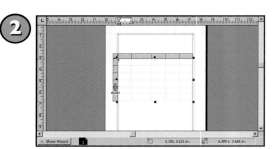

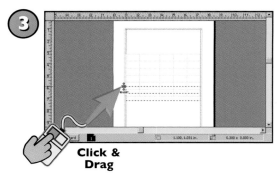

✓ Using Grow to Fit Text

If you are changing row heights in anticipation of typing several lines of text into a particular row's cell (which would require more height), don't bother. Just make sure that the **Grow to Fit Text** command is selected on the **Table** menu. Then the row's height will change automatically (become greater) as needed, when you type the text.

Click & Drag

1 Click on the table to select it.

2 Place the mouse pointer on the row divider below the row you want to size.

3 Drag to increase or decrease the height of the row.

4 Release the mouse button.

Task 6: Inserting Rows

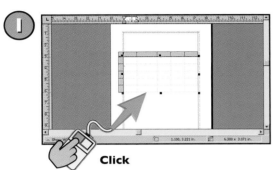

Click

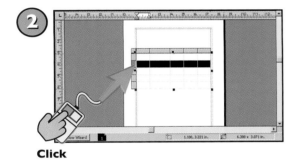

Click

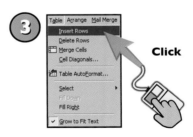

Click

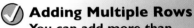

Adding Rows to the Table

If you find that you need additional rows in the table, you can easily add them. You can add one or more rows, depending on the number of new rows you need. All you have to do is select a row or rows by clicking on the row selector (the box on the left side of the row).

Adding Multiple Rows
You can add more than one row to the table at a time. Click and drag on the row selectors to select the number of rows you want to insert into the table. Use the **Insert Rows** command on the Table menu to insert the new rows.

Undoing Row Additions
If you find that you've added the new row or rows at the wrong position in the table, click the **Undo** button to quickly remove the new rows.

---

1. Click on the table to select it.

2. Click a row selector to select it.

3. Choose **Table**, **Insert Rows**. The new row is inserted below the selected row.

Task 7: Inserting Columns

Adding Columns to the Table

You can also add new columns to the table. Select a particular column or columns, and then the new column or columns will be added to the right of those selected.

Start Here

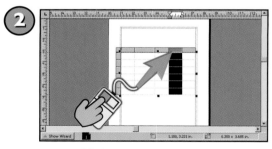
Click

✓ **Adding Multiple Columns**
Remember to select the same number of existing columns as the number of new columns you want to add to the table.

✓ **Resizing the Table**
When adding columns or rows to a table, you will find that this action makes the table and its frame larger as well. Because the limiting factors on a regular (8 1/2 by 11 inches) page are the left and right margins, you may have to resize tables you add additional columns to.

Click

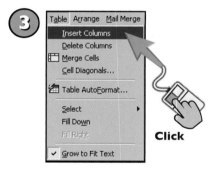
Click

1 Click on the table to select it.

2 Click a column selector to select the column.

3 Choose **Table**, **Insert Columns**.

End Task

Task 8: Removing Rows

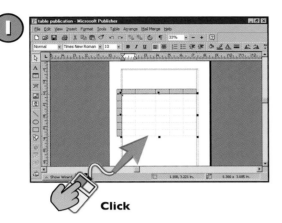

Click

Deleting Table Rows

You can easily delete rows you don't want in your table. You can delete a single row or select several rows and then remove them.

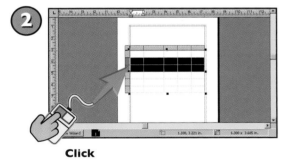

Click

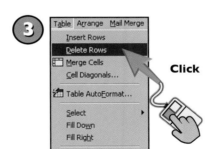

Click

1. Click on the table to select it.

2. Use the row selectors to select a row or rows for deletion.

3. Choose **Table**, **Delete Rows**.

✓ **Deleting a Row and Its Contents**
If you delete a row or rows that contain text, you also delete the text (the contents) of the row.

Task 9: Removing Columns

Deleting Table Columns

Deleting columns from the table is as easy as removing a row or rows. You merely select the columns you want to delete and then remove them using the Delete Columns command.

Click

✓ **The Delete Key Doesn't Remove the Columns**

You must use the **Delete Columns** command to actually remove the columns from the table. If you want to remove only the contents of a selected column or columns, you can press the **Delete** key on the keyboard.

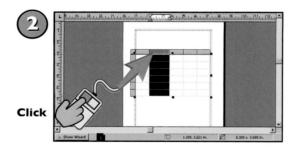

Click

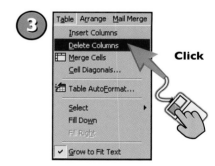

Click

1 Click on the table to select it.

2 Use the column selectors to select a column or columns for deletion.

3 Choose **Table**, **Delete Columns**.

Task 10: Dividing Cells on the Diagonal

Start Here

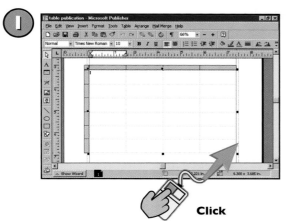

Click

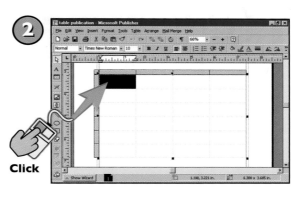

Click

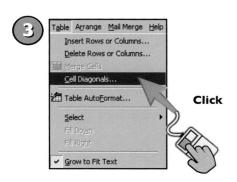

Click

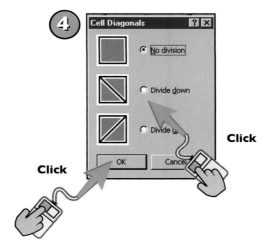

Click **Click**

Inserting a Diagonal in a Cell

You can divide a cell on the diagonal, making the cell, in effect, two different cells. This approach is particularly useful if you are creating a schedule or a calendar. For instance, it's not uncommon to have two dates listed on a particular calendar day (for example, 24/31).

✓ **Entering Text in the Divided Cell**
To enter text in a cell divided on the diagonal, click below the line and then enter text at the insertion point. You can then click above the diagonal line and enter text in that area as well.

✓ **Using the Diagonal to Delineate Empty Cells**
You can also divide a cell on the diagonal to denote that cell as empty or as a "do not use" cell.

1. Click on the table to select it.

2. Drag to select a cell or cells that will be split on the diagonal.

3. Choose **Table**, **Cell Diagonals**.

4. In the Cell Diagonals dialog box, select **Divide down** or **Divide up**, and then click **OK** to close the dialog box.

End Task

Task 11: Merging Table Cells

Removing Column Dividers by Using Merge Cells

You can take several cells in the same row and make them one continuous cell. Then you could place text all the way across the row because it exists as just one cell. This is very useful for placing a heading at the top of a table or dividing a table into different parts.

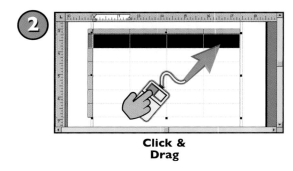

Click & Drag

✓ Centering a Heading in Merged Cells

The first row of a table makes an excellent place to type a heading. Because the entire row is one merged cell, you can center the heading text by clicking the Center button on the Formatting toolbar.

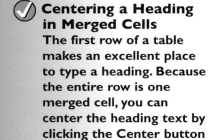

Click

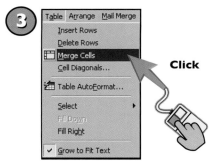

Click

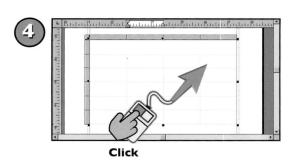

Click

✓ Splitting Cells

You can also split cells that have been merged. Select the merged cell and choose **Table, Split Cells**. The original number of cells will be created from the selected merged cell.

① Click on the table to select it.

② Drag to select the cells you want to merge.

③ Choose **Table**, **Merge Cells**.

④ Click anywhere in the table to deselect the merged cells.

End Task

Task 12: Entering Text in a Table

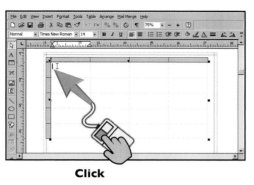

Click

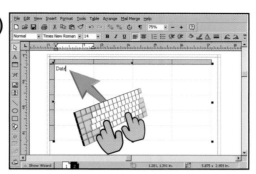

Filling Your Table with Information

After you've created a new table, you can quickly enter text into the table cells. After entering your text, you can format the text by using any of the text attribute tools discussed in Part 3, "Changing How Text Looks."

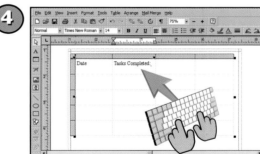

 Moving in the Table
You can quickly move forward a cell by pressing **Tab**. The **Shift key + Tab** takes you back a cell. The up- and down-arrow keys move you quickly up or down a cell.

 Formatting Text
Select any text attributes you want to use for the text before you begin typing in the cells. That way all the cells share the same text formatting.

1. Click in the first table cell you want to enter text in.

2. Type the text for the first cell.

3. Press the **Tab** key to move to the next cell.

4. Enter the text for this cell.

Task 13: Using the Table AutoFormat

Formatting the Table Automatically

You can format a table quickly by using one of the AutoFormats provided by Publisher. These AutoFormats provide you with text formatting, cell color formatting, and various other formatting attributes. The AutoFormat feature is a great way to create eye-catching tables for your publications.

✅ Reformatting with AutoFormat

If you don't like your AutoFormat choice, you can repeat the task steps and select a new look for your table.

✅ Formatting AutoFormatted Items

You can change the format on individual items in the table (such as text) that have been formatted by AutoFormat. Select the text and then use the Formatting toolbar to select a particular font, font size, color, or other attribute.

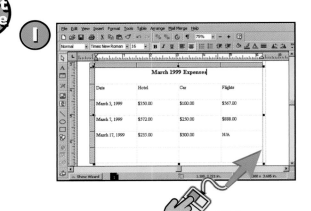
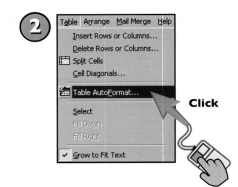
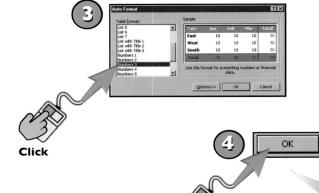
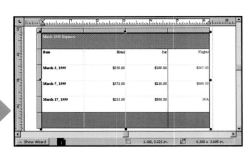

Start Here

Click

Click

Click

Click

1. Click on the table to select it.

2. Choose **Table**, **Table AutoFormat**.

3. Choose a format for the table from the list provided.

4. Click **OK**. The table is formatted.

End Task

Task 14: Manually Adding Colors and Borders to a Table

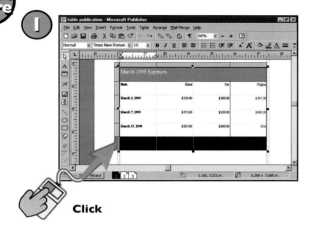

Click

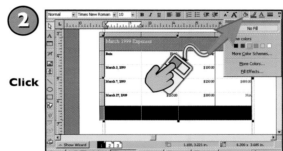

Click

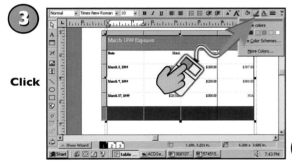

Click

Formatting the Table Manually

If you would rather format the table border and fill colors manually, you can use the Line Color and Fill Color buttons on the Formatting toolbar to selectively format the table.

---

1. Select a cells or cells to format.

2. Click the **Fill Color** button on the Formatting toolbar, and select a color for the cells.

3. Click the **Line Color** button on the Formatting toolbar, and select a border color for the cells.

4. Click anywhere on the publication to deselect the cells.

✓ Formatting Tables and Cells Is Like Formatting Frames

Adding borders to your table or adding borders and fill colors to cells involves the same techniques you used to enhance frames with borders and colors. See Part 5, "Working with Frames," for more information on working with borders and fill colors on frames.

End Task

Page
127

Enhancing and Printing Your Publications

After you spend a lot of time designing a publication, you will want to print a hard copy of the final product or ready the material for printing by a commercial printing service. Publisher offers several tools that allow you to fine-tune your publication and get it ready for the printer.

Tasks

Task 1: Using Color Schemes

Changing Your Color Scheme

As you get your publication ready for printing, you may want to take a final look at the color scheme you've selected for a publication. How you use colors and the scheme you select will definitely influence the overall feel and impact of the publication. You can easily switch entire color schemes in Publisher and then switch them back if you want.

✓ Creating a Custom Color Scheme

You can also create a custom color scheme in the Color Scheme dialog box. Choose the **Custom** tab in the dialog box. Use the **Scheme colors** drop-down boxes on the left side of the tab to set the custom colors for each element of the publication. To save your new color scheme, click the **Save Scheme** button. Type a name for the new scheme and then click **OK**.

Start Here

Click

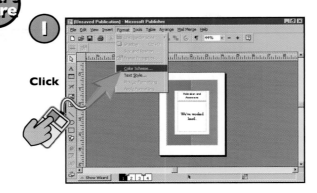

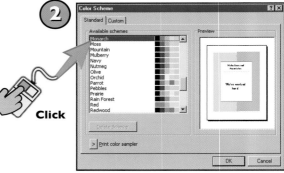

Click

3 OK

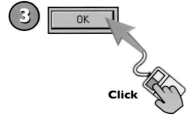

Click

1 With the publication open in the Publisher window, choose **Format**, **Color Scheme**.

2 In the Color Scheme dialog box, choose a new color scheme in the Available schemes box. A preview of the scheme appears in the Preview box.

3 After you've selected the new color scheme you want to use, click **OK** to return to the publication.

End Task

Task 2: Using the Spelling Feature

Start Here

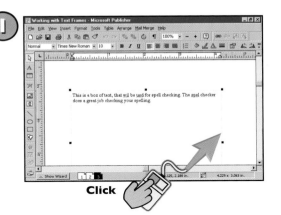

Click

Click

Catching Typos in Your Publications

Before printing a publication you should use the handy Spelling feature which checks your documents for misspellings and typos.

✓ **Choices in the Check Spelling Dialog Box**
When a suspected misspelling appears in the Not in Dictionary box you can choose a correct spelling in the suggestion list and click **Change**, ignore the word by clicking **Ignore**, or click **Add** to add the word to the dictionary file.

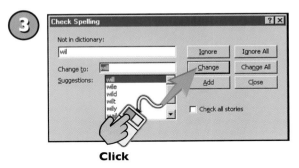

Click

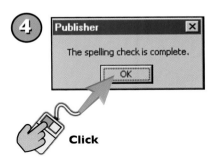

Click

✓ **Suspected Misspellings Are Flagged as You Type**
Publisher will flag misspellings as you type. A red, wavy line appears under the flagged word. When you see this you can immediately Right-click on the word and select a correct spelling from the list provided on the shortcut menu that appears.

1. Select the text frame you want to spell check.

2. Choose **Tools**, **Spelling**, **Check Spelling**.

3. In the Check Spelling dialog box, select a correct spelling for the word displayed in the Not in Dictionary box, and then click **Change** to correct the Word.

4. Correct other suspected misspellings. When the Spelling feature has completed checking the publication, click **OK**.

End Task

Task 3: Using the Design Checker

Checking Your Publication's Design

The Design Checker is another great tool for helping you fine-tune your publication before printing. The Design Checker actually looks at the design elements and objects in your publication and helps you find empty frames, improperly proportioned pictures, font problems (such as too many), and other design problems. The great thing about the Design Checker is that it offers you help when it identifies a potential design problem.

✓ **Fixing Design Errors**
The Design Checker will flag suspected design problems in your publication. In many cases the Design Checker will not be able to fix the problem for you (as the Spelling feature can) but will explain to you what it thinks the potential design flaw is. You can then close the Design Checker and fix the problem.

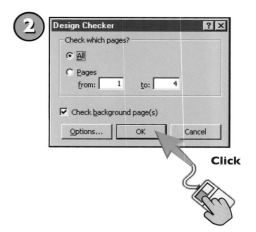

Click

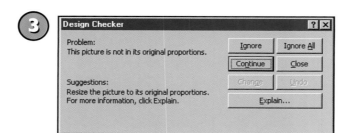

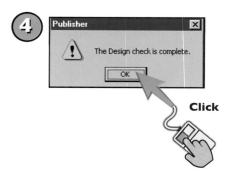

Click

Click

1   Choose **Tools**, **Design Checker**.

2   In the Design Checker dialog box, specify which pages you want checked, and then click **OK** to start checking the publication.

3   If an error is found, click the appropriate choice in the Design Checker dialog box to ignore the problem, change it (if available), or to continue.

4   When you have checked the entire publication (and either ignored or fixed the flagged design problems), the Publisher dialog box appears; click **OK** to close it.

Task 4: Working with Hyphenation

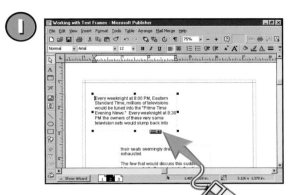

Click

Click

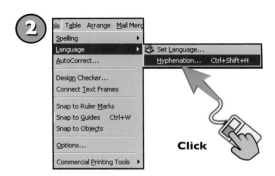

Click

Automatically Hyphenating Words in Text Boxes

You can have **Publisher** automatically hyphenate the text in your text boxes (meaning that it determines where to break a word). The really great thing about the feature is that if you edit the text, unnecessary hyphens are removed (automatically) and new hyphens are placed as needed.

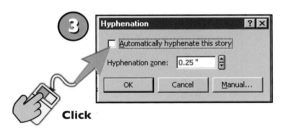

Click

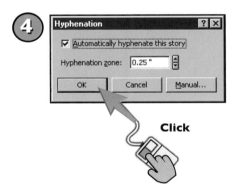

Click

(✓) **Manually Hyphenating Text**
To manually hyphenate the text in a text box, choose **Tools, Language, Hyphenation.** In the Hyphenation dialog box, click **Manual.** A dialog box appears, containing the first word to be hyphenated. **Click Yes** to accept the hyphen; click **No** to reject the hyphen.

(1) Choose the text box you want to automatically hyphenate.

(2) Choose **Tools**, **Language**, **Hyphenation**.

(3) Click the **Automatically hyphenate this story** check box in the Hyphenation dialog box.

(4) Click **OK** to exit the dialog box and hyphenate the text.

Task 5: Using Color Matching

Matching Monitor and Printer Colors

As you ready a publication for printing, you will want to make sure that the colors that are actually printed by the printer are the same as or at least very close to the colors you saw on your monitor as you designed the publication. To aid the printer in matching the colors on the computer monitor, you can turn on the Color Matching feature.

✓ **Some Printers Don't Provide Color Matching**
Depending on the printer you have attached to your computer, you may not have the option of turning on the color-matching feature in the Advanced Print Settings dialog box. The option will be grayed out. This is true for black-and-white–only printers such as laser jets.

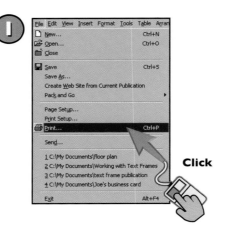

Click

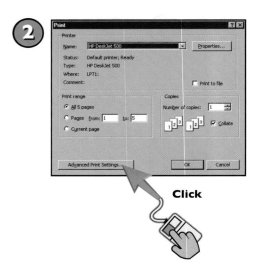

Click

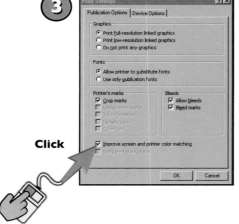

Click

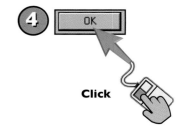

Click

Start Here

1 Choose **File**, **Print**.

2 In the Print dialog box, click **Advanced Print Settings**.

3 Click the **Improve screen and printer color matching** check box.

4 Click **OK** to close the dialog box and return to the Print dialog box.

End Task

Task 6: Printing the Publication

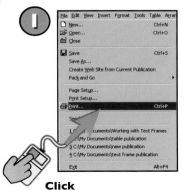

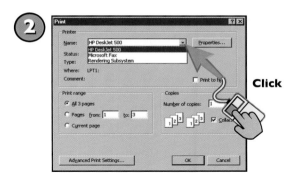

Click

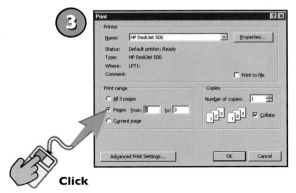

Click

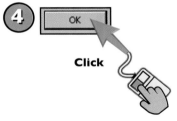

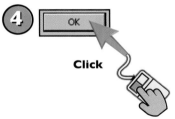

Click

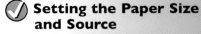

Click

Getting Your Publication to the Printer

No matter how hard you work on the color and design parameters of your publication, the final judge of your skills will be how the publication appears on the printed page. **Publisher actually does a very good job of printing both full-color and black-and-white (grayscale) publications.**

(1) Choose **File**, **Print**.

(2) If necessary, click the **Name** drop-down box and select the printer you want to send the print job to.

(3) Click the appropriate radio button to print a page range or the current page.

(4) Click **OK** to send the print job to the selected printer.

Setting the Paper Size and Source

Before you print, you may want to set the paper size you are using and the printer bin you placed the paper in. **Choose File, Print Setup.** Set up paper-related options as needed, and then click **OK**.

Troubleshooting Printing Problems

On the rare occasion that your text doesn't look right, a portion of a picture is cut off, or the printer won't print the publication at all, you can call on the Print Troubleshooter.

☑ **Try and Try Again**
If a Print Troubleshooter solution does not alleviate your current problem, try opening the Troubleshooter again and use a different solution. Also try printing from another application (make sure that your printer is turned on, plugged in, and securely attached to your computer).

☑ **Getting the Most out of Help**
The Publisher Help System provides you with a great deal of easy-to-access information related to all aspects of creating your publications. See Part 1, "Getting Started with Publisher 2000," for more information on using the Help system.

Task 7: Using the Print Troubleshooter

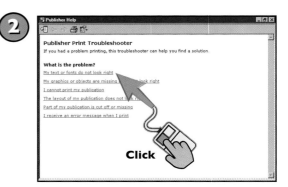

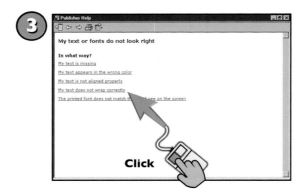

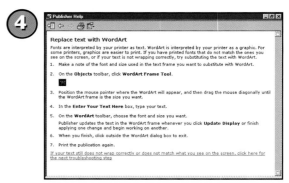

① Choose **Help**, **Print Troubleshooter**.

② The Help window appears on the desktop. Choose one of the print troubleshooting topics in the Help window (for example, **My text or fonts do not look right**).

③ Then, a second, more specific level of help topics appears. Choose a selection to view the help associated with it.

④ Help is provided to specifically remedy the problem you selected. Click the **Close** button to close the Help window.

Task 8: Using Pack and Go

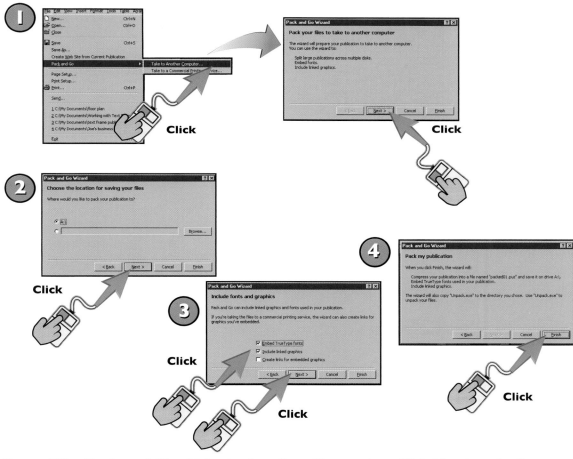

Click

Click

Click

Click

Click

Click

Taking Your Publication on the Road

The more pictures, text frames, and various design elements in a publication, the larger the file size. Luckily, you can compress large publications using *Pack and Go*, then take your publication to another computer or to a commercial printer.

✓ Unpacking to Multiple Disks

If the packed publication will not fit on one floppy disk, the Pack and Go Wizard prompts you to place additional disks in your **A:** drive.

✓ Unpacking the Publication

A copy of Unpack.exe is placed on the disk with your packed presentation. Use this program to unpack your publication onto another computer. Place the disk in the other computer, choose **Start, Run**. In the Run box type `a:\unpack.exe`.

1. Choose **File**, **Pack and Go**, **Take to Another Computer**. Click **Next** on the first screen to start the Pack and Go Wizard.

2. To pack the publication to a disk, click **Next** (or specify another drive on your computer and then click **Next**).

3. To embed the fonts and pictures in the publication in the Pack and Go file, click the appropriate check boxes, and then click **Next**.

4. Click **Finish** to pack the publication onto a disk.

Task 9: Using the Commercial Printing Tools

Setting Up a Publication for Commercial Printing

The commercial printing tools in Publisher help ready a publication for printing by a professional printer. Two of the most important aspects will be selecting the appropriate color scheme (so that it matches the printer) and saving embedded pictures and graphics as separate files linked to your publication (a necessity if you use a professional printer).

✓ Changing from RGB Colors to Process or Spot Colors

Computers use RGB as the standard color printing system. For color publications printed by a printing service, you will want to have the publication printed using process colors (especially if photos are included). For publications needing only one or two additional colors, select *spot colors*.

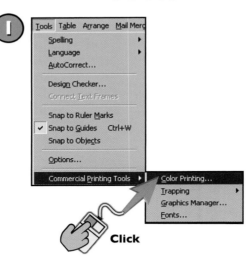

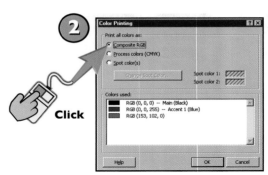

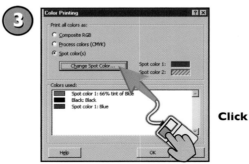

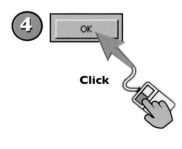

1. Choose **Tools**, **Commercial Printing Tools**, **Color Printing**.

2. In the Color Printing dialog box, click the radio button for the color scheme specified by the printing service you will use.

3. If you select Spot Colors, click the **Change Spot Color** button to edit any of the currently selected colors.

4. Click **OK** to close the dialog box.

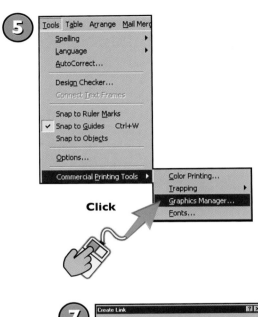

Click

Click

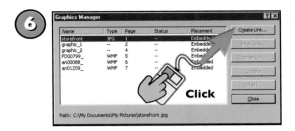

Click

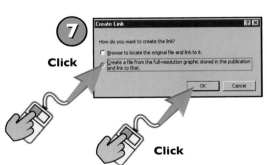

Click

Click

Click

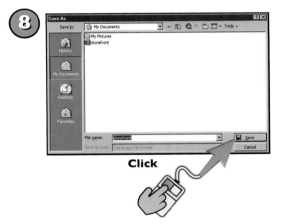

Click

Linking Graphics to the Publication

Your pictures and clip art inserted on publication pages is called *embedding*. When you have a publication printed by a commercial service, you often must provide the pictures and clip art images as separate files that are linked to the publication rather than embedded in it. The Commercial Printing Tools option provides a Graphic Manager that allows you to convert your embedded objects to linked objects before you take the publication to a printing service.

Pack and Go Packs the Linked Graphics
You can use Pack and Go to compress the entire publications (including linked graphics)into one file to give to the professional printing service.

⑤ Choose **Tools**, **Commercial Printing Tools**, **Graphics Manager**.

⑥ In the Graphics Manager dialog box, choose the first picture or clip art item in your publication, and then click **Create Link**.

⑦ In the Create Link dialog box, click the **Create a file** radio button. Click **OK** to create the linked file.

⑧ Click **Save** in the Save As dialog box, and the linked file is saved. Create other links as needed for your graphics files.

End Task

Using Advanced Publisher Features and Creating a Web Page

Publisher provides some slick advanced features that can really help you create great-looking presentations. For instance you can create text stories that allow text to flow between text frames. You can also perform a mail merge in Publisher, which allows you to create one publication and then merge it with addresses and names for mass mailings. Publisher also helps you create your own Web site for use on the World Wide Web.

Tasks

Task 1: Creating Story Frames

Flowing Text Between Frames

You can take text and have it flow between several text frames on a publication page or pages. The text is called a *story*. Your story can flow between as many text frames as you like, and the amount of the story that resides in a particular text frame will depend on the frame size.

✓ **Creating Text Frames**
You create text frames by using the **Text Frame Tool** on the Publisher toolbar. For general help with text frames, see Part 3, "Changing How Text Looks."

✓ **Full Frames Display an Overflow Indicator**
When you have more text than the text frame can display (because of its size), an overflow indicator appears at the bottom of the text frame.

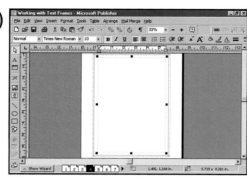

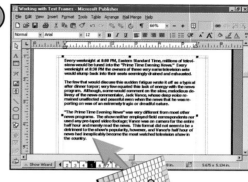

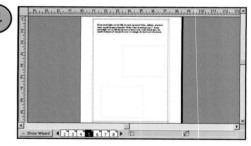

① Create a text frame that can contain the entire story.

② Type the entire text story into the text frame.

③ Size the text frame so that only the part of the story that you want to show in that frame appears.

④ Create the other frames that will hold the rest of the story text.

Next Step

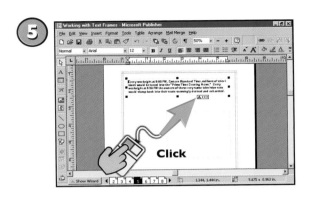

Click

Click

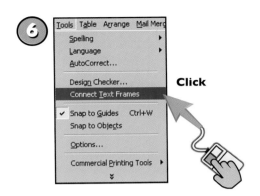

Click

Flowing the Text to Other Frames

After your story text has been sized in the first text frame, you can create other text frames that will hold the rest of the story. These text frames can be on the same page or other pages of the publication.

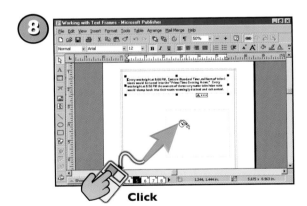

Click

Click

✅ **Completing the Text Flow**
After the text flows to the next text frame, it will show an overflow indicator. Use steps 7 and 8 to flow the text into the next empty frame you've created, and continue this process until all the frames are filled.

✅ **Making Sure There's No Overflow on the Last Frame**
When you flow the text, make sure that the last frame in the connected story frames does not have an overflow indicator. This means that all the text in the story is displayed in the frames.

⑤ Click on the text frame that holds the text.

⑥ Choose **Tools**, **Connect Text Frames**.

⑦ Click the **Connect Text Frames** button that appears on the Standard toolbar.

⑧ Click the pitcher icon on the next (empty) frame that will hold the story.

End Task

Task 2: Inserting a Text File

Using Text Files Created in Other Applications

Because Publisher is geared toward publication design, you might find that for long text entries, it's easier to create a text file in another application, such as Windows WordPad or Microsoft Word, and then insert the text file into your publication.

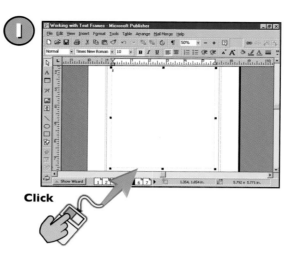

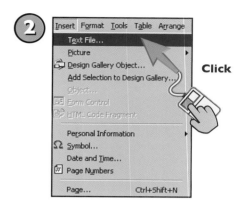

✅ **Inserted Text Files Make Great Stories**
Inserting long files into Publisher makes it easy to create stories that flow between several text frames.

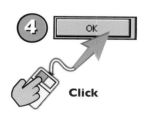

✅ **Publisher Supports Many Text File Types**
Publisher allows you to insert files saved in various formats, including Word .doc files, text files created with Notepad, and other file formats.

① Create a text frame to hold the inserted text file.

② Choose **Insert**, **Text File**.

③ In the Insert Text dialog box, locate the file you want to insert and select it.

④ Click **OK** to insert the file into the current text frame.

Task 3: Selecting Special Page Layouts

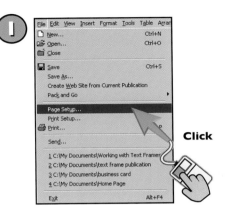

Click

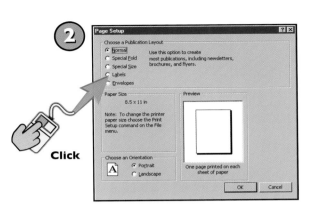

Click

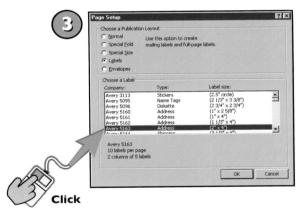

Click

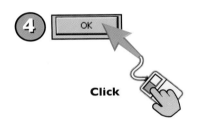

Click

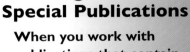

Working with Special Publications

When you work with publications that contain folds (such as brochures) or that print on special paper (such as mailing labels and envelopes), you will want to set up the page layout so that it accommodates your special publication.

(1) Choose **File**, **Page Setup**.

(2) Click the appropriate radio button to select your page layout (such as **Labels**).

(3) Choose the appropriate paper or label type from the list provided (such as an Avery label type).

(4) Click **OK** to close the dialog box.

⚠ **Warning**
If you designed your mailing label or envelope using a Wizard, the Wizard has already selected the page setup based on your choices. Don't change the page layout for these publications, or they may not print correctly.

Task 4: Creating a Publisher Mailing List

Building a Mailing List

If you want to send a particular publication to various people, you can create a *mailing list*. Publisher has a merge feature you can use to personalize the publication for each person on the list.

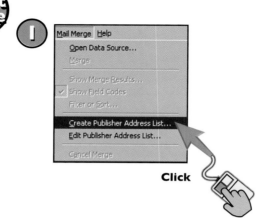

Click

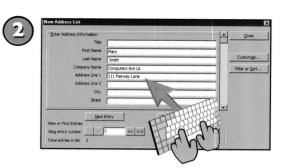

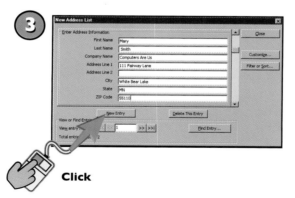

Click

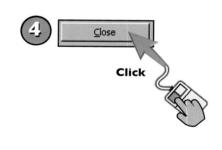

Click

① Choose **Mail Merge**, **Create Publisher Address List**.

② Type the appropriate information for your first addressee in the New Address List (press the Tab key to move to the next field).

③ Click **New Entry** to enter the next person.

④ Click **Close** when you have entered all the names and addresses.

Next Step

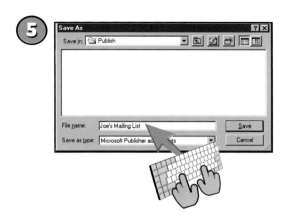

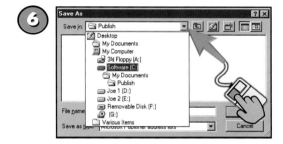

Click

Saving Your Mailing List

After you have entered all the names and addresses into your Publisher Mailing list, you need to save the mailing-list file. Publisher saves the file in a database format (.mdb, the same format used by Microsoft Access, the database program).

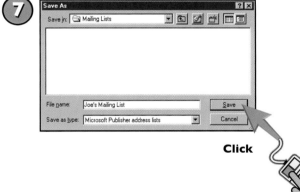

Click

5 Type a name for your mailing list file.

6 Select the drive and folder where you want to save the file.

7 Click the **Save** button.

 Using Other Data Sources

If you use **Microsoft Access** and have already created a table of names and addresses for your contacts, you can use it as your mailing list for merges with **Publisher** publications.

End Task

Task 5: Editing a Publisher Mailing List

Adding or Removing Data from the Mailing List

You will probably find that the information in your mailing list changes over time. You might need to add more names and addresses, edit an address, or remove a person from the list.

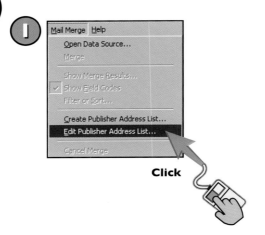

Click

Click

Start Here

Deleting an Entry

You can remove an entry from the mailing list. Use the **Forward (>>)** or **Previous (<<)** buttons on the bottom of the Mailing List dialog box to locate the entry for a particular person. Click **Delete This Entry** to remove the entry.

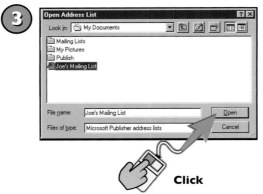

Click

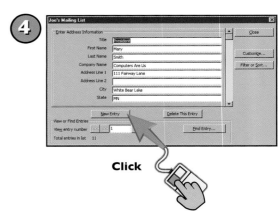

Click

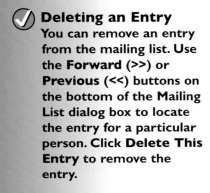

1. Choose **Mail Merge**, **Edit Publisher Address List**.

2. Select the mailing-list file in the Open Address List dialog box.

3. Click **Open** to open the list.

4. To add another entry, click **New Entry**. Then add the appropriate information.

Next Step

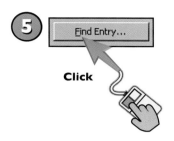

Click

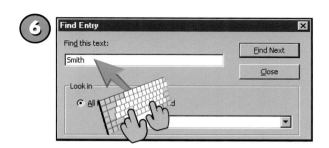

Finding Specific Entries

Because you may need to edit a specific entry in the mailing list, you can forgo looking through all the entries (a real pain if there are a lot of people) to find the person by using the Find Entry button. You can then edit or remove the entry.

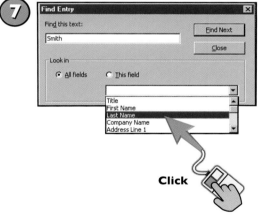

Click

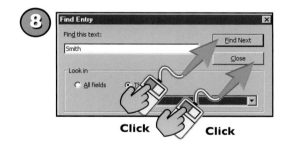

Click   **Click**

Closing the Mailing List

When you close the edited mailing list, changes you've made to the mailing-list file are saved. If the Publisher dialog box appears, asking you to save changes, click Save to save the changes to the publication and the mailing list.

(5) Click the **Find Entry** button.

(6) Type a text entry in the Find this text box that will be used to find the entry (such as the person's last name).

(7) Click the **This field** radio button and specify the field that the text will be found in.

(8) Click **Find Next** to find the entry. When finished, click **Close.**

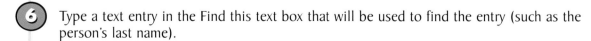

Task 6: Setting Up a Merge

Preparing the Publication for the Merge

After you've created a mailing list, you need to place *merge codes* into the publication. These codes are placeholders for information that will be pulled from the mailing-list file. For instance, to place the first name of a person in the merged publication, you need to enter the First Name code into the publication.

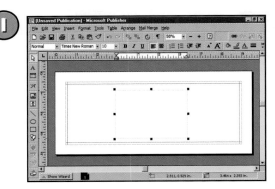

Click

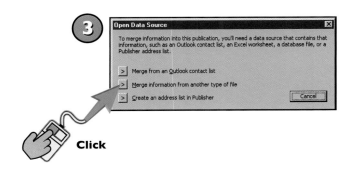

Click

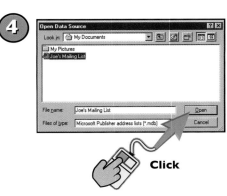

Click

✓ Creating a Mailing List On-the-Fly

If you don't already have a mailing-list file for the merge, click **Create an address list in Publisher** in the Open Data Source dialog box, and create a list for the merge.

(1) Open the publication (such as a mailing label or an envelope), and create a text box to hold the merge codes.

(2) Choose **Mail Merge, Open Data Source**.

(3) Click **Merge information from another type of file**.

(4) Select your mailing-list file and click **Open**.

Next Step

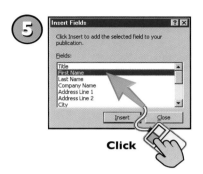

Click

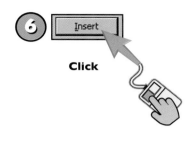

Click

Inserting the Merge Codes

After opening the data source for the merge, you can insert the merge codes into the publication. The merge codes are inserted into a text box on the publication page. After the merge codes are inserted, you can perform the merge.

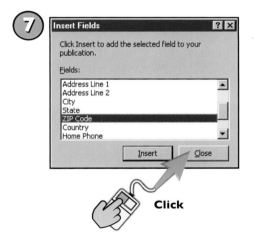

Click

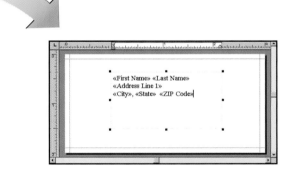

«First Name» «Last Name»
«Address Line 1»
«City», «State» «ZIP Code»

(5) Select a merge code in the Insert Fields box.

(6) Click **Insert** to insert the appropriate code.

(7) Insert other codes as needed, and then click **Close**.

✔ Adding Spaces and Punctuation to the Merge Codes

After you insert a code, such as first name, click in the text box and press the spacebar before you insert the last name code. You can also use this technique to insert punctuation between merge codes, such as the comma between city and state.

End Task

Task 7: Performing a Merge

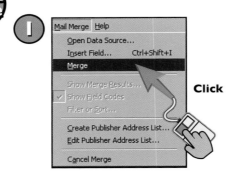

Click

Creating the Merged Publications

After you've created a mailing list and then inserted the merge codes into a publication (in a text frame), you are ready to perform the merge. After previewing the merge results, you can send them to the printer, where the publication will print a page for each individual in your mailing list.

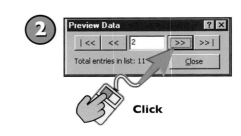

Click

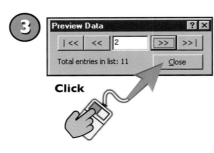

Click

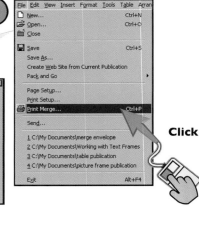

Click

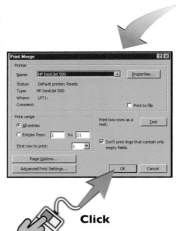

Click

✅ Stopping the Merge

If you find that there is a problem with the merge when you preview your entries, choose **Mail Merge, Cancel Merge.** You can then edit the mailing list or publication and try the merge again.

① Choose **Mail Merge**, **Merge**.

② Click the **Next Record** button on the Preview Data dialog box to view more data.

③ Click **Close** when you are done previewing the merge.

④ Choose **File**, **Print Merge** to print the merged publications. To print, click **OK**.

Task 8: Creating a Web Site

Click

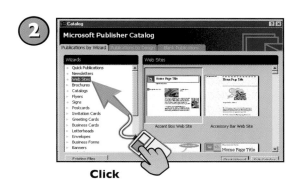

Click

Making Your Own Web Page

Publisher can help you create your own Web site without your having to know the *HTML* coding language. The Web Site Wizard walks you through all the steps necessary to create a great-looking Web page for use on the *World Wide Web*.

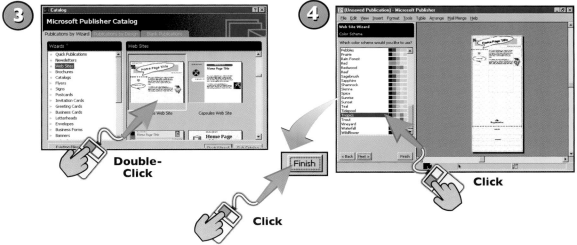

Double-Click

Finish

Click

Click

Click

✓ **Editing a Web Site**
You will want to edit the placeholder text that is placed in the Web site publication. Select the text and change it as needed (for more about working with text, see Part 3 of this book).

✓ **Adding Objects to a Web Site**
You can add pictures, text frames, and other objects to your Web site just as you would for any other publication type.

1. Choose **File**, **New**.

2. Click **Web Sites** in the Wizards pane.

3. Double-click a Web site style in the Web Sites pane.

4. Make your color and design selections with the Web Site Wizard, and then click **Finish**.

Task 9: Adding Hyperlinks

Inserting Hyperlinks into a Web Site

A *hyperlink* is a link to another Web site or another page on your own Web site. Hyperlinks can take the form of text entries or pictures. Click them and you are taken to a new location. You can use any object you insert on your Web page as a hyperlink.

✓ **Creating Links to Your Web Pages**
If you have a Web site consisting of multiple pages, you can create links to these pages. Click **Another page in your Web site** (in the Hyperlink dialog box), and then specify the appropriate page.

✓ **Adding Hyperlinks from Your Favorites List**
If you've added Web sites to your Favorites list when using the Internet Explorer Web browser, add these sites as hyperlinks by clicking the **Favorites** button in the Hyperlink dialog box.

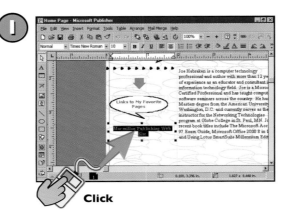

Click

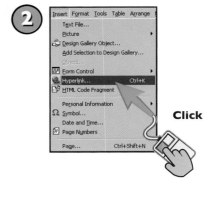

Click

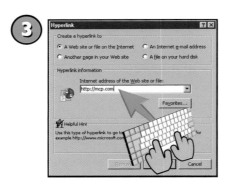

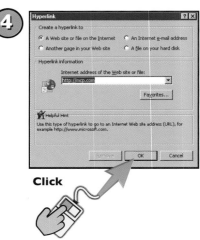

Click

1 Select any object on your Web page, such as a picture, a text frame, or text in a text frame.

2 Choose **Insert**, **Hyperlink**.

3 Type the name of the Web site.

4 Click **OK**.

Task 10: Removing Hyperlinks

Start Here

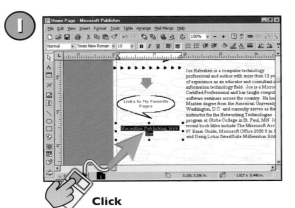

Click

Click

Click

Removing Hyperlinks from a Page

You can also remove a hyperlink from a text entry or a picture on your Web page. This action doesn't remove the object; it only takes away its hyperlinking capabilities.

① Select the text in a text frame or another object on the Web page that contains the hyperlink.

② Choose **Insert**, **Hyperlink**.

③ Click the **Remove** button.

✓ **Hyperlinks Help You Create Compact Web Pages**
Although you might think that a Web site with a lot of information on it negates the need for hyperlinks, you should keep in mind that Web pages containing short text entries and visual objects provide more impact. Use hyperlinks to move the reader from page to page rather than concentrating the text all in one place.

End Task

Task 11: Previewing a Web Site

Viewing Your New Web Site

After you've setup your Web site, you can preview it in the Microsoft Internet Explorer Web browser. This lets you make sure that the hyperlinks and other objects look good and work correctly.

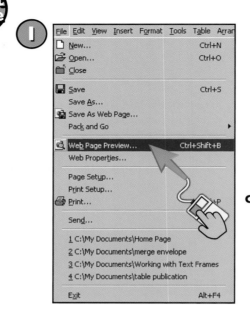

Click

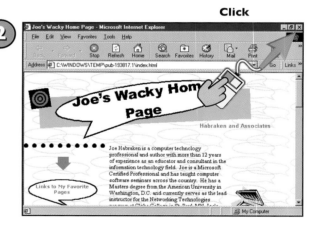

Click

✓ **Fine-Tuning Your Web Site**

If you connect to your Internet service provider, before previewing the Web page, you can actually test the hyperlinks in the Web page and see whether they connect appropriately.

1 Choose **File**, **Web Page Preview**.

2 After previewing your Web site, click the **Close** button to close Internet Explorer.

Task 12: Publishing a Web Site

Start Here

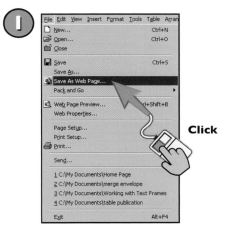

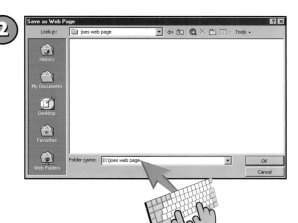

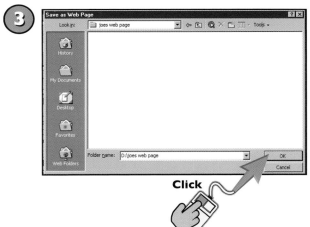

Click

Saving Your Web Site to a Folder

Web Sites consist of text, pictures, hyperlinks, and various other items such as sound files and video clips. When you have completed the creation of your Web site, all these elements must be saved to a folder on your computer. The items in this folder can then be uploaded to a *Web server* that places your site on the World Wide Web.

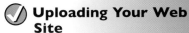
Click

1. Choose **File**, **Save As Web Page**.

2. Type a folder name or specify a folder by using the mouse.

3. Click **OK** and the Web site is saved to the folder.

✓ Uploading Your Web Site

For your Web site to be available on the World Wide Web, it must be placed on a Web server, which is a computer that "serves up" Web pages to people using a Web browser. Contact your *Internet service provider* for information on uploading your Web page to a Web server.

End Task

background The area that exists behind the pages of a publication. If you need items to be repeated on all your publication's pages, such as the page number, place them in the background of the page; these items will then appear on each page.

border The delineating outside line of a frame or an object in a publication. You can change the line thickness and color of the border.

cell The intersection of a row and column in a table of information where you will place your data. A table makes it very easy to arrange information in a highly organized format.

drop cap An enlarged and bolded first character that emphasizes the beginning of a paragraph of text. The drop cap feature separates the first capital letter from the normal paragraph text, providing you with a nice design element to begin a text block.

embedding Placing pictures or clip art on a publication page. Before having a publication professionally printed, you may need to convert the object images to linked files rather than embedded ones. See also *linked*.

facing pages The pages that appear side-by-side in an open publication.

font The overall look and shape of typed text is determined by its character style or typescript. Fonts come in a wide variety of appearances; the text you type in a new text frame will be created in the default Publisher font, which is Times New Roman, 10 point. You can easily change the font for new text or text that already exists in a text frame.

footer An item, such as a page number, that repeats at the bottom of every page of a publication.

foreground Items not in the background. When you place various frames and other items on your page, you are working in the foreground of that page. See also *background*.

frame The delineated area that an object resides in. You can format frame borders, change the color of frames, and manipulate frames in various ways.

grid guides Nonprinting vertical and horizontal guidelines used to line up and position the various items you place on a page. Grid guides appear on every page, no matter what page you create them on. See also *ruler guides*.

header An item that repeats near the top of every page of a publication.

HTML Hypertext Markup Language. HTML is the programming language that Web sites are written in. Publisher's Web Site Wizard can help you create your own Web site without having to know HTML.

hyperlink A link to another Web site or another page on your own Web site. Hyperlinks can take the form of text entries or pictures. Click them and you are taken to a new location.

input device A hardware device, such as a scanner or digital camera, that captures images you can place in your publications.

Internet service provider The company that provides Internet service to your home or office computer for a fee. Internet service providers typically set you up with a connection to the Internet so that you can take advantage of the World Wide Web, and they also provide you with an email account.

linked When embedded objects, such as pictures or clip art, are converted so that they become separate files that are attached to the publication. Commercial services typically require linked objects in order to print your publication. The commercial printing tools provide a Graphic Manager that lets you convert your embedded objects to linked objects before you take the publication to a printing service.

mailing list The list of people (and their addresses) indicating who you want to send your publication to. You can create the list in Publisher and merge it with the publication to personalize the mailing for each person on the list.

merge code Placeholder for information that will be pulled from the mailing-list file. For instance, to place the first name of a person in the merged publication, you need to enter the First Name code into the publication.

object Any item—such as a picture, text box, logo, calendar, or coupon—you add to your publication pages. Publisher provides a great deal of help when it comes to placing objects in your publications. The Publisher status bar and rulers are designed to help you place and size your objects appropriately.

OLE Object linking and embedding. Lets you place objects created in other applications into your publication. For instance, you can place an Excel Worksheet and a chart into a publication, or you can place a PowerPoint slide on a page. These types of objects are often referred to as OLE objects. See also *embedding* and *linked*.

Pack and Go A method of compressing your publication files so that you can transport them easily. The Pack and Go feature compresses your publication and lets you place the compressed file on one or more disks.

Page Width view Allows you to zoom in on the publication page but still see the left and right margins. It is a useful page view because it provides a view (58%) that is slightly larger than zooming to 50% while maintaining the total width of the page.

personalized menu A menu system, in Microsoft Office 2000, that adapts to your usage. Your most-recently used commands appear at the top of each respective menu.

placeholders Generic objects placed in a Wizard-created publication that you can replace with your own pictures or with other objects.

process color A color printing mode that uses four color channels: cyan, magenta, yellow, and black. Process colors are used by printing service bureaus to print multicolor publications, especially those that include photographs.

publication The end product of your work in Publisher. A publication can be a flyer, a brochure, a set of business cards, or any number of business or personal documents with special looks and layouts.

Publisher Catalog A listing of design choices that appears when you open Publisher, letting you begin a new publication by using a Publication Wizard, a Design Set, or a template.

ruler guides Nonprinting vertical and horizontal guidelines used to line up and position items you place on a page. Ruler guides appear only on the page where you create them. See also *grid guides*.

server application The software application in which an embedded object was created. When you place OLE objects on your publication pages, you can edit them in their original server application by double-clicking on the object. See also *OLE*.

shortcut menu A menu that appears when you right-click on any object on the publication page.

smart object Logos, mastheads, and other specially designed objects that Publisher provides for you through a set of Wizards in the Design Gallery. Smart objects can be edited at any time with the appropriate Wizard.

Snap to Object A built-in feature that makes it easy to align objects to another object. For instance, you can drag a text frame to a particular position on the page and place it near another object, and it will automatically snap to the object and align itself.

spot colors A professional printing term for coloring publications that use only one or two colors. Spot color is used for black-and-white publications that also use a color or two for highlighting and emphasis on the pages.

story Text that flows between several text frames on a publication page or pages.

style Specific attributes, such as the text size, color, and alignment, that are saved and assigned to selected text. For instance, you may want to make the text in several text frames bold, italic, 12 point, and centered. Rather than assigning each attribute one at a time to the text, you can create a style that can do all the formatting at once by applying all the attributes to selected text.

template A model publication, containing basic layout and formatting, that you can use to base a new publication on.

text frame An object that will contain text in your publication. Text frames are created with the Text Frame tool on the Publisher toolbar.

Two-Page Spread view A whole-page view that allows you to examine two facing pages in relation to each other. Two-Page Spread view can be turned on from the View menu.

Web server A computer (usually owned by your Internet service provider) that makes your Web-page site available on the World Wide Web and then "serves it up" to people using a Web browser.

Whole Page view A bird's-eye view that is excellent for determining the overall layout of the page and the positioning of the various text frames, picture frames, and other objects.

Wizard A special software feature that walks you through the steps of creating publications or various objects in Publisher.

World Wide Web A global group of interconnected computers that store Web pages. Web browsers help you navigate through the many Web pages available.

A

B

C

cropping pictures

P

Q-R

S

selecting

U

W

zooming in/out

X-Y-Z

Notes

Get **FREE** books and more...when you register this book online for our Personal Bookshelf Program

http://register.quecorp.com/

 Register online and you can sign up for our *FREE Personal Bookshelf Program...*unlimited access to the electronic version of more than 200 complete computer books — immediately! That means you'll have 100,000 pages of valuable information onscreen, at your fingertips!

 Plus, you can access product support, including complimentary downloads, technical support files, book-focused links, companion Web sites, author sites, and more!

 And, don't miss out on the opportunity to sign up for a *FREE subscription to a weekly e-mail newsletter* to help you stay current with news, announcements, sample book chapters, and special events including sweepstakes, contests, and various product giveaways!

 We value your comments! Best of all, the entire registration process takes only a few minutes to complete...so go online and get the greatest value going—absolutely FREE!

Don't Miss Out On This Great Opportunity!

QUE® is a product of Macmillan Computer Publishing USA—for more information, please visit: *www.mcp.com*